Incidents in the Life of

Cecilia Lawton

MERCER UNIVERSITY PRESS

Endowed by

TOM WATSON BROWN
and
THE WATSON-BROWN FOUNDATION, INC.

Incidents in the Life of

Cecilia Lawton

A Memoir of Plantation Life, War, and
Reconstruction in Georgia and South Carolina

Edited by KAREN STOKES

Preface by James E. Kibler, Jr.

MERCER UNIVERSITY PRESS
Macon, Georgia
MMXX

MUP/ H996

© 2021 by Mercer University Press
Published by Mercer University Press
1501 Mercer University Drive
Macon, Georgia 31207
All rights reserved

25 24 23 22 21 5 4 3 2 1

Books published by Mercer University Press are printed on acid-free paper that meets the requirements of the American National Standard for Information Sciences—Permanence of Paper for Printed Library Materials.

Printed and bound in the United States.

This book is set in Adobe Caslon Pro and Georgia (display).

Cover/jacket design by Burt&Burt.

ISBN978-0-88146-765-9

Library of Congress Control Number: 2020948221

Complete Cataloging-in-Publication Data is available from the Library of Congress

Contents

Acknowledgments

It was Dr. James E. Kibler who first pondered the whereabouts of Cecilia Lawton's memoir and urged me to seek it out; therefore, much credit must go to him for this endeavor and for the fine preface he has contributed. Another person who deserves thanks is Jill Hunter Powell, the able director of the Confederate Museum in Charleston, South Carolina. She was the key to finding the memoir because she put me in touch with a collateral descendant of Cecilia Lawton, Anna Lebby Campbell, who kindly and generously allowed me to borrow the original document. I am grateful to her for permitting me to transcribe and edit Cecilia's work. Others I must thank include author and historian Jim Hayes, who allowed me to use an unpublished manuscript in his collection; Doug Bostick, an authority on James Island history; and Vernon Edenfield, pastor of the Little Ogeechee Baptist Church in Oliver, Georgia.

Preface
Art from Tragedy

The knowledge that the world has of Cecilia and Wallace Lawton comes largely from two books published by Algonquin Press— Clyde Bresee's *Sea Island Yankee* (1986) and *How Grand a Flame: A Chronicle of a Plantation Family, 1813–1947* (1992). The latter tells the story of three generations of the Lawtons and their plantation where Bresee was a child and son of the plantation dairy manager from Pennsylvania. In *How Grand a Flame*, the publisher included an illustration of a page from the manuscript of Cecilia Lawton's diary-memoir, which Bresee made the primary source for his volume. Bresee had retold the incident pictured in the page reproduced from Lawton's manuscript—but comparison showed his version to be an inaccurate paraphrase. This discrepancy made me curious to see if there might be other such inaccuracies in Bresee's volume. Events have proved the suspicion correct. *How Grand a Flame* and the recovered Lawton manuscript tell very different stories.

Bresee's book spurred me to contact Karen Stokes in early 2018 to see if she might be able to locate Lawton's manuscript. In a rapid series of happy events coupled with some detective work, Mrs. Stokes was able to locate the manuscript. This occurrence yielded a fortuitous bonus. Included with the newly discovered manuscript was a copy of the page proofs of *How Grand a Flame* upon which the descendant-owner of the manuscript, Mrs. Lavinia R. Campbell (who loaned it to Bresee), pointed out Bresee's additions and inaccurate reportings. It was clear that she was not pleased with the way Bresee used the manuscript she loaned him. Her extant annotated proof copies revealed that she attempted to get Mrs. Lawton's story reported more accurately. Bresee conjectured conversations and fabricated scenes, but he omitted other sentences and situations that would cast a favorable light on both the Lawtons and their society. In one instance, Mrs. Campbell noted that Bresee added words and quoted them as if they were Cecilia Lawton's own, but they are nowhere to be found in her manuscript. Bresee removed a few of the most blatant distortions that she pointed out to him, but the book remained more a fictive imagining than authentic history.

The result was that despite Mrs. Campbell's recommendations, Bresee's portrayal stayed the same: this family, especially its men, were violent, cruel, and boorish. He was not subtle in depicting Southern society as inferior to his own Northern world, to which he and his family returned in 1930 owing to events occasioned by the Depression. In *Sea Island Yankee*, Bresee admits that his family was treated well on James Island and in Charleston, but the book's overall negative view of the Lowcountry suggested to me a possible reason he might have manipulated the diary the way he did. Reading *Sea Island Yankee* prompted me to redouble my efforts to see that the Lawton manuscript was published, so that these radically different portrayals of the Lawtons would be available for the reader to compare. Such comparison might yield future interesting conclusions concerning the Lawtons, their biographer, and the nature of scholarship on the South in our time.

The result of this complicated odyssey is that the reader now has Cecilia Lawton's own carefully edited manuscript without conjecture, deletions, or additions, so that the reader may experience her story in her own voice. Her narrative is the record of a strong and resilient couple enduring the horrific conditions imposed by war, invasion, and brutal conquest. In places, it corroborates the many accounts of General Sherman's war on civilians and gives new eyewitness details about some events of that campaign. As an eyewitness testimony to Sherman's campaign to and from the sea, Lawton's diary is an important historical record, but it is more than that. It reveals her to be a very gifted writer. The artistry with which Lawton narrates her personal experiences makes it riveting reading.

Mrs. Lawton's graphic descriptions of the "pestilential" stench from the rotting carcasses in the mass slaughterings of all the animals in the country—a smell so noxious that civilians had to move away—are nowhere more memorably recorded in the annals of the war. Her portrayals of the suppurating corpses of ex-slaves left unburied where they fell by the wayside following the Federal army, and the rotting corpse of a blue-clad white U.S. soldier by the wheel tracks of the road she was travelling—and all being feasted upon by flocks of buzzards—are likely to etch themselves in the reader's memory, as they did Mrs. Lawton's. She writes, "The recollections, even now, sicken me. The country was one vast region of *silence, desolation* and *death*!"

The accuracy of her descriptions is proved by George Ward Nichols, aide-de-camp to Sherman himself, in his *History of the Great March*. Nichols, in fact, uses similar words to describe the army's path: "Where our footsteps pass, fire, ashes and desolation follow." He declares he feels no pity for civilians' "cries for help," "wails of pain," and "faces pale with fear."[1] Nichols quotes Sherman as saying that killing off the African American camp followers has become a "favorite hobby of mine."[2] It is possible that some of the corpses of these unfortunate men and women were among those whom Mrs. Lawton saw and described. Again corroborating the accuracy of Mrs. Lawton's unforgettable descriptions of "desolation and death" are Nichols's own boasts of the army's thorough work of destruction in the counties through which it passed: "Our work has been the next thing to annihilation."[3] Nichols also quotes the incendiary general as saying that the South's "best blood" has been killed on the battlefield, but there is still "a class of persons at the South who must be exterminated."[4] Mrs. Lawton would find words like "annihilation" and "extermination" all too accurate in detailing the devastation she witnessed. As shown

[1] Nichols, *History of the Great March*, 140.
[2] Ibid., 119.
[3] Ibid., 81.
[4] Ibid., 171, 119.

through the record of her personal experiences, the war is no longer an abstraction, or total war merely a strategy. In the process, her narrative approaches art, and often art of a high nature. It is not surprising to find that Mrs. Lawson wrote and published poetry.

Another example of her artistry is the well-written, memorable scene in which a desperately hungry Cecilia and her husband, Wallace, are trying to make a meal in the ashes of their home surrounded by miles of scorched landscape. They look at each other over the inedible mess and burst into laughter at the ludicrousness of the picture. One will likely appreciate Mrs. Lawton's saving sense of humor at the lowest and scariest of times.

How families like the Lawtons endured as they did—and what they did—still amazes me. The scene in which Cecilia and Wallace face down the drawn bayonets of the United States occupation troops is artfully drawn as a lesson in fortitude. Some of the soldiers threaten them with the gory details of how they have split the heads of their victims with axes, but the couple is not intimidated—or at least they show no sign of it. Wallace, certainly an imperfect individual, is as heroic as his wife. At times both he and Cecilia display nobility in affliction. During Reconstruction, he manages to make a living for the family by sheer force of will, rebuild without complaining, and help his wife on the way to wealth sufficient for her to buy and operate Charleston's Mills House Hotel in 1901.

For his efforts, Wallace is forced to leave his beloved farm on James Island in old age, much to his deep consternation and regret, and to live in an apartment at the hotel. He obviously shared his wife's sense of humor in bad times. He calls the hotel a "hot hell," and an unnatural "box with people below and above." He was plantation born and bred and loved the peaceful spring mornings on the farm, which had an unblemished, unobstructed view of the distant spires of the city across the Ashley River. He liked the smell of the newly ploughed soil. He missed the community of farmers and the camaraderie of the James Island Agricultural

Society. City life, even in so pleasant a place as Charleston, was simply not to his liking. Still he soldiered on with a kind of gruff and curmudgeonly sophistication that traditional Southerners are likely to appreciate. He died in the hotel in 1906.

One of the tragedies of the Lawton chronicle is that after all of Wallace Lawton's heroic struggles to survive on the land of his ancestors, where they had been stewards since the early 1700s, he ends up trapped in a "box" in the city, divorced from the fields he loved, those fields which, in the words of his wife "yielded kindly and saved our land from greater and widespread starvation." Cecilia sees to it that their son goes to VMI rather than the Citadel. This only surviving child marries a woman from Virginia who is not a farm woman and they have no children. This wife "from off" survives her husband and as a widow sells the family farm on James Island in 1947. It subsequently becomes a housing development in 1951 and an early part of Charleston's suburban sprawl west of the Ashley River. The extended story may thus be interpreted as a full-blown agrarian tragedy affecting more than this one family. In his version of the Lawton saga, Bresee appears to appreciate none of this or explore its root cause.

If one looks for lessons in the Lawton saga, as Bresee often does, there are plenty. The antebellum Lawtons, despite the faults families are heir to, are survivors. They survive by intelligence, strength of character, and the will to live and carry on despite seemingly insurmountable obstacles and impossible circumstances. Their early story is a chronicle of endurance and a testament to the abiding strengths of the traditional culture's devotion to family and place, the record of which Cecilia Lawton has bequeathed to future generations through memorable art. How grand a flame, indeed!

James Everett Kibler, Jr.
Ballylee, September 2018–February 2020

Editorial Note

In transcribing Cecilia Lawton's memoir, I made few changes except for spelling out abbreviated words. Also, in a few instances, I added punctuation to sections that included quotations from her diary in order to distinguish them as diary entries. Cecilia's large, angular handwriting has its idiosyncrasies, but the work is largely quite readable in the original. Much of the memoir is written in faded brown ink, and its lined, numbered pages are contained within sturdy hardback covers measuring eight by ten inches and decorated with marbleized paper.

Cecilia's memoir was likely handed down in the family to her great-niece Anna Royall Lebby (1884–1971), the granddaughter of Anna Lawton Oswald (Cecilia's sister). Mrs. Lebby then passed it on to her niece Lavinia Estelle Royall Campbell, whom she helped to raise after the death of Lavinia's father, Calhoun Clark Royall, in 1944. Lavinia, who was always called Dinnie, passed away in 1993, and her husband, Robert A. Campbell, has kept the memoir since then. His daughter, Anna Lebby Campbell, was kind enough to allow me to use the Lawton memoir.

In 2018, when Anna Campbell loaned me the original manuscript of Cecilia's memoir, she also loaned me the "advance uncorrected proofs" of Bresee's book *How Grand a Flame*. Lavinia (Dinnie) Campbell, who found some of his work and opinions objectionable, had marked it with numerous comments and requests for deletions. Bresee had included quoted from several nineteenth- and twentieth-century historians, all of whom wrote disparagingly of the South, especially its planter class. Among the historians quoted was Page Smith, who opined, "Above all the South was a world of violence. With all the surface show of gentility and refinement, violence lay at its heart."[5] At Mrs. Campbell's request, Bresee deleted some of these derogatory remarks—

---

[5] Smith, *Trial by Fire*, 17.

including Smith's and another by Henry Adams. However, Bresee maintained his contention that many, if not most, Southern slave owners were characterized by a "love of violence" and were somehow more violent and cruel than other men, ostensibly offering Winborn Wallace Lawton as evidence.[6] Lawton had, after all, punished some of his slaves with beatings and had fatally shot a relative during a dispute. Bresee, however, offered no condemnation of the widespread and well-documented violence and savagery of Sherman's operations in South Carolina, which he simply described as "systematic and supererogatory."

---

[6] Bresee, *How Grand a Flame*, 166.

Introduction

Cecilia Lawton was born in 1847. Fourteen years later, in 1861, the bloodiest war in American history began, and her life as the daughter of a wealthy Georgia plantation owner was forever changed. Cecilia married at the age of sixteen and went to live at her husband's plantation in South Carolina, but a few months later, she found herself fleeing from the army of General William T. Sherman as it embarked on a path of destruction across the state. She also observed the aftermath of this brutal campaign in Georgia and South Carolina, writing of what she saw with her own eyes in vivid, horrific detail.

In 1992, author Clyde Bresee made use of Cecilia's writings in his book *How Grand a Flame*. It received mostly positive reviews although one reviewer for *Publishers Weekly* criticized it for "frequent arguable conjectures." Bresee drew heavily from Cecilia Lawton's "diary" (which was in fact a memoir into which she had transcribed parts of a diary) and quoted a number of passages directly from Cecilia's work, but her memoir has never been published in its entirety until now. Writing in the latter part of the 1870s, or possibly later, she gave it the title "Incidents in the Life of Cecilia Lawton." Its last page, numbered 212, covers events in 1872, and it appears that she meant to continue her narrative, but the rest of the 352-page journal is blank. What we have of this unfinished work, however, is an intriguing and sometimes shocking glimpse into the civilization of the antebellum South, the cruel and devastating war that crippled it, and the tragic struggles of its people in the postwar period.

Cecilia was the daughter of Robert Themistocles Lawton (1807–1881) and Harriet Charlotte Singleton Lawton (1807–1863), both of whom were natives of Beaufort District, South Carolina, a coastal district south of Charleston. Robert T. Lawton was born in Robertville, but his family later made their residence in a nearby village, Lawtonville, founded by his father. After their marriage, Robert and Harriet lived in Georgia, residing in a house on Habersham Street in Savannah for many years before moving about sixty miles northwest to Screven County in the early 1850s.

The antebellum South was an agrarian society, and Screven County, Georgia, established in the late eighteenth century, was no exception. In 1855, the Rev. George White published a documentary history, *Historical Collections of Georgia*, in which he wrote that there were nearly 500 farms in in Screven County, which had a population of 3,173 white persons and 3,673 slaves. Most of these farms were small, producing crops of cotton, corn, and sweet potatoes, and, along the rivers, rice. Large herds of sheep and cattle were also raised. The town of Sylvania, often mentioned in Cecilia's memoir, was created as the new county seat in 1847. Soon afterward, a courthouse was built there, and the town grew rapidly. The Lawton plantation was located about three miles north of Sylvania.

In the latter part of the 1850s, the Lawton family led a somewhat nomadic existence. Robert moved them around a number of times while he worked supervising railroad construction in southern Georgia, but in early 1860, he returned to planting in Screven County and forever gave up railroad building. "Indeed," observed Cecilia, "he promised his slaves never to engage in it again, for they were not as comfortable as when at their houses, where they had all their crops, chickens, pigs and some cows."[7] He began building a new, larger house on his plantation in late 1860, but the blockade of Southern ports the following year prevented him from obtaining all the materials he needed, giving rise to its name, Blockade Place. Although the residence was not fully completed according to plan, it was livable, and the Lawton family moved into this new home in spring 1862.

Cecilia's memoir, of course, notes the "momentous events" that occurred in South Carolina in December 1860 and the first

---

[7] Lawton, "Incidents in the Life of Cecelia Lawton," 28.

half of 1861. Up to the day of the bombardment of Fort Sumter on April 12, 1861, the whole nation had been watching and waiting to see if the crisis brought on by U.S. troops occupying this fort in Charleston Harbor would lead to war.

Prior to South Carolina's secession from the union in December 1860, a delegation of South Carolina congressmen had communicated with outgoing U.S. president James Buchanan; they believed they had reached an agreement that the federal government would not try to reinforce its forts in South Carolina or make any change in their status. However, in the last week of December 1860, Major Robert Anderson, the commander of a small garrison of federal troops at Fort Moultrie on Sullivan's Island, secretly moved all his men to Fort Sumter in the middle of the night. His soldiers spiked the cannons at Fort Moultrie and set the gun carriages on fire upon their departure. The governor of South Carolina regarded their stealthy seizure of Fort Sumter and the sabotage of Fort Moultrie as an act of war, so, in response, the South Carolinians took possession of the federal arsenal in Charleston as well as a small harbor fort called Castle Pinckney.

In January 1861, another event took place which South Carolina viewed as a hostile act. The U.S. government sent a civilian freighter, *The Star of the West*—with armed troops and munitions concealed below deck—to Charleston in a furtive attempt to reinforce Fort Sumter. The South Carolinians found out about this "secret" mission and knew that the ship was not simply a harmless civilian vessel. South Carolina artillerists first fired a warning shot before the ship was fired upon in earnest, which caused it to reverse course and depart.

Other states followed South Carolina in seceding from the union, and in February 1861, the Confederate States of America was formed in Montgomery, Alabama. The following month, Abraham Lincoln was inaugurated as president of the United States.

While all this was going on in the winter and spring of 1861, Cecilia was a student at the Orangeburg Female Academy in

Orangeburg, South Carolina. When school was over in June, she returned to Blockade Place in Screven County. Her memoir records all the changes that affected her family because of the war over the next few years, but one of the most touching sections of this part of her narrative deals with the death of her mother, Harriet Singleton Lawton, a model wife and plantation mistress known for her many acts of benevolence and charity. Cecilia described her as a "Blessed, saintly Christian woman! Gentle, refined, Southern lady! Kindly friend, mistress and neighbor, devoted, *most devoted* wife and mother—all of these and much more she was, as all who knew her can testify."[8]

Anyone who has read Margaret Mitchell's novel *Gone with the Wind* will notice a similarity between Harriet Lawton and Scarlett O'Hara's devout, benevolent mother. Just as Scarlett admired Ellen O'Hara, honoring her as a great lady ("the embodiment of justice, truth, loving tenderness and profound wisdom"), Cecilia Lawton revered her own "angel mother" and aspired to her example, expressing the ardent wish, "Oh! that I might be like unto her, even in the smallest degree."[9]

Poignantly recounting her mother's last hours, she related how, the day before her death, Mrs. Lawton had embraced and kissed Cecilia many times, calling her "by the sweetest & most endearing terms." Early the next morning, Cecilia was summoned to the deathbed where her mother lay unconscious. Mrs. Lawton soon passed away quietly and peacefully, surrounded by her family and household servants, by whom she was deeply mourned. Cecilia wrote,

> The house and yard was full of wailing negro slaves who had left their work in the fields and hastened from every part of the plantation upon hearing of the approaching calamity. As the breath left the beloved body, their sobs and wails suddenly became louder, for several of the older women had even

---

[8] Lawton, "Incidents," 86.
[9] Mitchell, *Gone with the Wind*, 63.

entered her room, where we all stood around her bed. These humble friends and slaves bemoaned her loss and repeated over and over to each other her numerous kindnesses to them.

Harriet Singleton Lawton died in August 1863. Less than a year later, in June 1864, to the great surprise and dismay of his children, Cecilia's father remarried, and his new bride promptly made it known that her stepchildren were no longer welcome in their own home. About this time Cecilia and her sister Georgia visited their married sister, Anna Oswald, in McPhersonville, South Carolina, a village in Beaufort District where Anna's husband, Robert, was stationed with Kirk's Cavalry and other Confederate forces. When these troops were ordered elsewhere, Cecilia and her sisters went to Lawtonville, and it was there that she met her future husband, Winborn Wallace Lawton, a distant cousin from the Charleston area. He was in Beaufort District, she explained, as a refugee who had "recently bought a large plantation near Lawtonville (six miles off) and moved his slaves there, having been ordered to remove them from James Island by the Confederate Government in charge. He called upon us with one of our cousins, almost immediately after our arrival, and began paying me constant attentions at once." Wallace, as he was called, was twenty-seven years old at the time—eleven years her senior—and was temporarily out of the army due to a recent illness.

Unsure of her feelings for Wallace, Cecilia was not easily persuaded into an engagement, but he was extremely persistent and persuasive, and within about two months of their first meeting, on September 20, they were married. They went to live at his plantation near Lawtonville, but before their honeymoon was "scarcely over," Wallace resumed his Confederate military service. He enlisted in a company of reserves under the command of E. H. Peeples and also reportedly served as a scout in the 3rd South Carolina Cavalry Regiment under the command of Charles Jones Colcock (see Appendix 1).

While Cecilia remained on the plantation, her husband would come home for brief visits. Her other visitors included hundreds of hungry Confederate soldiers, most of whom she believed belonged to Wheeler's Cavalry. These soldiers, who were under the command of General Joseph Wheeler, were well behaved at the Lawton place, but they had a reputation for being undisciplined and plundering civilians. A recent book about these cavalrymen by John R. Poole, *Cracker Cavaliers*, asserts that, though there is no doubt that "isolated cavalry took what they needed from civilians," Wheeler's men were not responsible for "the worst of the depredations" attributed to them.[10] In a letter to Confederate president Jefferson Davis dated January 8, 1865, Wheeler's superior officer, General William J. Hardee, defended him, stating, "Wheeler's cavalry...is a well-organized and efficient body. The reports of its disorganization and demoralization are without foundation, and the depredations ascribed to his command can generally be traced to bands of marauders claiming to belong to it."[11] A biography of General Wheeler by John W. DuBose identified some of these marauders as enemy soldiers, claiming that a U.S. officer under the command of General James H. Wilson confessed that "the invading army had hundreds of their men distributed through the country, representing themselves as 'Wheeler's cavalry,' sent out on their work of theft and insult."[12]

Only a few months passed before the exigencies of war forced Cecilia to leave her new home. She fled to her father's plantation in Georgia, which had been partially destroyed by Sherman's soldiers. A history of Screven County published in 1989 contends there is strong historical evidence showing that relatively few houses were burned in this part of the state. The same history also states that enemy troops generally left behind a few days' worth of provisions at the farms and plantations where they foraged and pillaged.[13] If this was the general practice in Screven County, it

---

[10] Poole, *Cracker Cavaliers*, 172.
[11] Dubose, *General Joseph Wheeler*, 425.
[12] Dubose, *General Joseph Wheeler*, 421.
[13] Hollingsworth, *The History of Screven County*, 38–39.

was not always so in other places in Georgia. At Blockade Place, the house was not burned, but it was ransacked for valuables. Mills and other structures on the plantation were torched, and large amounts of livestock and foodstuffs were carried off or ruined. Soldiers also held a gun to the head of Cecilia's father to make him reveal the hiding place of "imaginary hoards of gold."[14]

Cecilia stayed at Blockade Place only briefly and then went on to Sylvania. In early 1865 she met two ladies who were refugees from Savannah, and there began what she called "one of the most unusual episodes of my life." The ladies told her that they had determined to return to Savannah disguised as "country crackers" (poor rural whites), and Cecilia decided to join them in this risky journey of about sixty miles.[15]

Moving toward the southeast, the three women left Sylvania and traveled by wagon to Whitesville (now called Guyton) in Effingham County. According to a recent history of Effingham County, it took five days for Sherman's troops to move through the town of Guyton in December 1864, leaving the surrounding area for miles around "devastated."[16] From Guyton, the ladies made their way into Chatham County, where Savannah is located. Cecilia recorded what she saw along their route "through a most desolated and ruined country, over which Sherman's brutal army had advanced in unchecked license only a few weeks before." Passing "scores upon scores of blackened chimneys," the three women saw no living animals, "but *hundreds*, yea, thousands, were seen lying dead and rotting on the roadside and in adjacent fields."[17] John T. Trowbridge, a newspaperman who toured parts of the South after the war, commented that the "deliberate aim" of Sherman's army in Georgia seems to have been "*to leave no stock whatever in the line of march*."[18]

---

[14] Lawton, "Incidents," 122.
[15] Ibid., 123.
[16] Renfro, *River to River*, 211.
[17] Lawton, "Incidents," 125.
[18] Trowbridge, *The South*, 478.

Cecilia and her companions also passed by the putrefying bodies of black men and a United States soldier in blue, and on two occasions, they saw "slaughter pens" of dead horses and mules. One of these pens was in a fenced graveyard next to a country church. Cecilia did not give the exact location, but it may have been the Little Ogeechee Baptist Church on the Old Louisville Road in Screven County, where some of Sherman's troops were briefly encamped. Another possibility is the Jerusalem Evangelical Lutheran Church in Effingham County. Wherever these pens were, they were filled with the rotting carcasses of the horses and mules taken from Georgia citizens or captured from Confederate troops and then slaughtered en masse by "inhuman Yankees."[19]

In her book *Through the Heart of Dixie*, Anne Sarah Rubin recounted several incidents of the mass killings of horses in Georgia by Sherman's troops. A resident of Butts County, J. A. McMichael, claimed that the soldiers slaughtered about a thousand horses taken from citizens and left the carcasses on an island in the Ocmulgee River. A similar story is also connected with the aforementioned Little Ogeechee Church. Here, in the church cemetery, General Sherman had penned some five hundred white horses he intended to take to Savannah, but then he decided they were not worth the trouble and ordered them shot. Even into the twentieth century, local residents recalled finding bullets embedded in some of the headstones.[20] In another incident, Union officer Smith D. Atkins recorded in his memoir that a cavalry brigade of his army had "captured hundreds of horses" in November 1864 after departing from Milledgeville. "The captured animals were a great incumbrance," he added, "and after each trooper had secured a good mount, over five hundred horses were killed by the Second Brigade."[21]

After Sherman's army had passed through Beaufort District in South Carolina, Cecilia and her husband returned to their

---

[19] Lawton, "Incidents," 126.
[20] Rubin, *Through the Heart of Dixie*, 51.
[21] Atkins, "With Sherman's Cavalry," 489–90.

plantation near Lawtonville, and upon their arrival, found that the house had been reduced to a heap of ashes and seven chimneys. Her heart nearly burst with grief and outrage as she gazed at these ruins, "so wantonly destroyed by a vindictive foe."[22]

Historian Thomas Bland Keys compiled an extensive (but by no means complete) catalog of Union excesses in his book *The Uncivil War*, observing,

> During the entire Civil War and early months of Reconstruction, wherever Federal forces—soldiers, marines, and sailors—went in the South, they inflicted terrorism on the inhabitants. Evil outrages were perpetuated by savage militants against women, children, old men, and Negroes—war waged on defenseless civilians. Many commanders issued numerous orders prohibiting such crimes, but only on rare occasions did a few even attempt to enforce these orders. Many commissioned officers, including generals, were among the guilty.[23]

The army of General William T. Sherman, with a force of over 60,000 troops, marched through Georgia in 1864 and South Carolina in 1865, burning farms, plantations, and towns; demolishing railroads; destroying or confiscating crops and livestock; and plundering and abusing civilians, black and white.

Sherman's army captured Atlanta in September 1864. Earlier, during the siege, Federal artillery had, without notice, deliberately directed fire over the Confederate lines of defense into the city itself, killing civilians there. Thomas J. Key, a Confederate soldier in Atlanta, recorded in his diary on August 23, "Not many days since, one shell killed a woman and her child while another poor child, who was lying in the bed sick, was struck by a shell and torn to pieces."[24] David P. Conyngham, a newspaper reporter traveling with Sherman's army, later observed that the city "had

---

[22] Lawton, "Incidents," 129.
[23] Keys, *Uncivil War*, 1.
[24] Cate, *Two Soldiers*, 119.

suffered much from our projectiles....Many of the citizens were killed, and many more had hair-breadth escapes."[25]

After his army occupied Atlanta, General Sherman ordered that its inhabitants must leave the city. The mayor and city councilmen begged him to reconsider because evacuating would cause suffering and hardship for the noncombatants, but the general refused. Weeks later, the army ended its occupation of the area and began its "march to the sea," leaving much of Atlanta in ashes. Other cities and towns in Georgia in its path would also suffer much destruction and pillage.

Describing the "foraging parties" of this army on the march, Conyngham wrote:

> They scattered over the country, without any order or discipline, pounced like harpies on the unfortunate inhabitants, stripping them of all provisions, jewelry, and valuables they could discover. In most instances they burned down houses to cover their depredations, and in some cases took the lives of their victims, as they would not reveal concealed treasure ... Many of our foragers, scouts, and hangers-on of all classes, thought, like Cromwell, that they were doing the work of the Lord, in wantonly destroying as much property as possible. Though this was done extensively in Georgia, it was only in South Carolina that it was brought to perfection.[26]

In December 1864, Sherman took possession of Savannah, Georgia. His next objective was the state of South Carolina, which was to be singled out for particularly savage treatment. In January 1865, in preparation for the invasion, many of his forces gathered at Beaufort, South Carolina, which had been in Union hands since November 1861. Some of Sherman's brigades began moving farther into the interior in January, and by the first of February, the main advance of the army had begun.

---

[25] Conynygham, *Sherman's March through the South*, 218.
[26] Ibid., 243, 266.

Dr. Henry Orlando Marcy, a Northern surgeon in a brigade under the command of Colonel Charles Van Wyck, recorded in his diary many observations about the operations of his brigade in Beaufort District and noted that on January 19, the 56th New York Infantry Regiment burned much of the village of Gillisonville, including the jail, a hotel, several houses, and a courthouse full of irreplaceable public records. Around this time, the nearby village of Grahamville was destroyed, and Hardeeville was partially burned, partially dismantled; soldiers took down buildings to make shelters for themselves. As they tore down Hardeeville's Baptist church, they taunted the townspeople, saying, "There goes your damned old gospel shop!"[27]

On January 31, the 15th Corps burned McPhersonville, and on February 5, 1865, the 14th Corps burned Robertville in Beaufort District. After Sherman's troops departed from Lawtonville, Cecilia's birthplace, there was nothing left except the chimneys of incinerated houses and a partially demolished church.

David P. Conyngham observed of the beginning of the South Carolina campaign, "There can be no denial of the assertion that the feeling among the troops was one of extreme bitterness towards the people of the State of South Carolina." Sherman's soldiers, he continued, were "eager to commence the punishment of 'original secessionists.' Threatening words were heard from soldiers who prided themselves on 'conservatism in house-burning' while in Georgia, and officers openly confessed their fears that the coming campaign would be a wicked one. Just or unjust as this feeling was towards the country people of South Carolina, it was universal." Every part of the state through which they passed, he added, "was converted into one vast bonfire." Comparing the campaign in Georgia to the one in South Carolina, Conyngham declared, "As for the wholesale burning, pillage, devastation, committed in South Carolina, magnify all I have said of Georgia fifty fold, and then throw in an occasional murder, 'just to bring an old,

---

[27] Elmore, *A Carnival of Destruction*, 50.

hard-fisted cuss to his senses,' and you have a pretty good idea of the whole thing."[28]

What has been called "the most monstrous barbarity of a barbarous march" was the destruction of Columbia, South Carolina, a city full of civilians, which had been surrendered by its mayor, only to be sacked and burned by Sherman's troops.

On January 4, 1865, a Charleston newspaper reprinted part of an editorial that appeared in the *Philadelphia Inquirer*, which cheered on General Sherman's troops as they began their campaign in South Carolina, "that accursed hotbed of treason."[29] In his book about Sherman, *Merchant of Terror*, John B. Walters commented, "This was a strange hatred which directed its venom not against armies but against the non-combatants of South Carolina and their personal property. The people of the North were, in effect, issuing an open invitation to the Union army to sack and pillage the country."[30] In December 1864, while he was in Savannah, Sherman told Mary C. West and her family that he had received letters from the "good, church going people of the North" urging him not to leave a house standing in South Carolina.[31]

Lawrence H. Keeley noted that General William T. Sherman's practice of total war "defied the rules and doctrines of Western civilized warfare."[32] Because of this, Sherman's operations in Georgia, the Carolinas, and elsewhere left a deep bitterness that lingered in the hearts of Southerners for many years. Walters commented that the bitter feelings of the people of the South "were intensified at the end of the war by the realization that so much of the widespread destruction which had been visited upon the civilian population by a vindictive enemy had been unnecessary for a Union victory."[33] Cecilia lamented in her memoir, "The ruin

---

[28] Conyngham, *Sherman's March*, 344.
[29] Quoted in Walters, *Merchant of Terror*, 190.
[30] Ibid., 198.
[31] West, "Statement in Reference to the Burning of Columbia," 2–3.
[32] Keeley, *War Before Civilization*, 177.
[33] Walters, *Merchant of Terror*, 206.

wrought by that one man, Sherman, in the Southern states will not be repaired in a 100 years, and some such as destruction of records, books & heirlooms, can never be made good."[34]

Regarding the thousands of slaves who had followed Sherman's army to Savannah, Walters noted, "The *Charleston Daily Courier*, January 31, 1865, quotes refugees from Savannah who stated that Negro women and children from the interior of Georgia were huddled together in a pen outside Savannah, where they were suffering from cold and exposure. Little, if any, food and clothing were supplied them by the Union army."[35]

When the war ended in April 1865, Wallace informed the workers on his plantation in Beaufort District that they were now free. Most of them were anxious to return to James Island, which they considered home, but he convinced them to stay at least until the end of the year so that the crops of corn and cotton could be harvested, having contracted with them to give them a third share. Some black soldiers, however, members of the United States Colored Troops, visited the Lawton plantation and told the sharecroppers that they did not have to work anymore—that "Uncle Sam" would give them plenty of food and take care of them.[36] The sharecroppers believed the soldiers, and all of them soon left the plantation bound for their home in Charleston District. "When we next saw them the following spring upon James Island," Cecilia remarked, "nearly all were pitted with smallpox marks, and had lost many members of their families."

The scourge of smallpox took the lives of thousands of former slaves during and after the war. According to recent scholarship, the worst outbreak in the Carolinas occurred in 1865, with a death toll of some 30,000 people.[37] Cecilia reported that during the summer and fall of that year, "500 negroes" succumbed to smallpox in a house on one of her husband's James Island plantations.

---

[34] Lawton, "Incidents," 129.
[35] Walters, *Merchant of Terror*, 242–43.
[36] Lawton, "Incidents," 147.
[37] Downs, *Sick for Freedom*, 106.

Unfortunately, Uncle Sam failed these people and many other freedmen in South Carolina and elsewhere. In his book *Sick from Freedom*, Jim Downs documented how the officials of the United States Bureau of Refugees, Freedmen and Abandoned Lands (commonly called the Freedmen's Bureau) proved ineffective in dealing with the epidemics that broke out among the newly emancipated slaves, who, according to Cecilia, called the pockmarks on their bodies "de Union mark."[38]

In September 1865, Wallace decided to sell some of his land near Lawtonville to his brother-in-law Asa Waring Lawton, but as the transaction was being finalized, the two men began arguing; the ensuing fight ended with Wallace shooting and killing Asa. After a trial, Wallace was acquitted of murder charges, but the episode was so painful for Cecilia that she could not bring herself to mention it in her memoir.

Later in 1865, while she was expecting her first child, her husband made a trip to James Island to "look after his property" there. He had been born and raised on this beautiful sea island, but he found it much changed after the war.

In his history of James Island, Doug Bostick noted, "James Islanders, white and black, faced incredible challenges after the end of the war."[39] J. Kersley Blackman, a Charleston newspaper correspondent, wrote of the island:

> It is directly opposite the City of Charleston, at the junction of the Cooper and Ashley rivers. It is half-moon shaped and is nine miles long, and varies in width from one-half mile to seven miles. It contains 12,000 acres, consisting of open fields, pine land, and dense thickets and swamps....In 1865 the proprietors of the soil returned to their plantations to find their houses destroyed and their lands in the possession of their former slaves. After much difficulty and loss of time the rightful owners recovered possession of their estates. In some instances, however, this was not accomplished until after three

---

[38] Lawton, "Incidents," 148.
[39] Bostick, *A Brief History of James Island*, 89.

years' delay. The planters were greatly impoverished, and having lost everything but their lands, it was hard, under the new order of things, and with the labor intensely hostile to their interests, for them to recover as rapidly as they might have done under more favorable circumstances.[40]

Wallace would also find Charleston much changed. A large part of the city was in ruins as a result of a terrible fire in 1861 as well as a lengthy, relentless bombardment from Federal artillery. Sidney Andrews, a Northern visitor who arrived in Charleston just after the war ended, described it as

> a city of ruins, of desolation, of vacant houses, of widowed women, of rotting wharves, of deserted warehouses, of weed-wild gardens, of miles of grass grown streets, of acres of pitiful and voiceful barrenness—this Charleston.... The beauty and pride of the city are as dead as the glories of Athens.... Now one marks how few young men there are, how generally the young women are dressed in black. The flower of their proud aristocracy is buried on scores of battle-fields.[41]

Even before the war ended, Charleston had been occupied by Federal troops. Uncertain as to whether General Sherman's army would descend on the city during his destructive campaign through the state, Confederate forces evacuated Charleston in mid-February 1865, and the place was left defenseless. Most of the residents also evacuated, and their unoccupied houses and other properties were left open to the depredations of the besieging Federal troops who immediately took possession of the city. For a long period after the war, the city was under military rule, and a number of houses and buildings were confiscated for the use of the occupation force and the Freedmen's Bureau. Most if not all of these properties were eventually restored to their former owners, but their contents were frequently missing, having been pillaged.

---

[40] Blackman, *Sea Islands of South Carolina*, 14.
[41] Andrews, *The South since the War*, 1–2.

Wallace had owned three plantations on James Island before the war, and upon his return discovered that all his property had been parceled out to freedmen. In time he was able to buy back the lands, but also found that it was difficult to find freedmen willing to work for him. In January 1866, Erastus W. Everson, an official with the Freedmen's Bureau reported that although the former slaves on the sea islands appeared to be "willing to work," they were "not willing to contract, under any circumstances." He further reported,

> In most cases, the Freed people, who now occupy these plantations, are not those who were formerly in bondage upon them, and I found discontent, and quarrelling, because the original workers of these places, upon their return, find that they are now being occupied by other Freedmen who have come up from the Country...most of the people who do come from the upper Counties, are those who are unwilling to make contracts there, and who have come to the Islands, and "squatted," with the intention of making crops for themselves alone.[42]

In his James Island history, Doug Bostick quoted another agent for the bureau, J. M. Johnston, who filed a report in 1866 asserting that there was "much idleness and vagrance" among the freed people on the island, and as a consequence, "they have made a poor crop generally." Johnston added that they were "gaining a livelihood by theft and robbery." In June 1866, General R. K. Scott, a commissioner of the Freedmen's Bureau in South Carolina, issued an order noting "the increasing amount of theft, drunkenness and vagrancy" among the freed people, and directing

---

[42] "Freedmen's Bureau Acting Subassistant Commissioner for Johns, James, Wadmalaw, and Morris Islands, South Carolina, to the Headquarters of the South Carolina Freedmen's Bureau Assistant Commissioner," 30 January 1866, Freedmen and Southern Society Project, University of Maryland, http://www.freedmen.umd.edu/Everson.html. Part of Hayden, et al., *Freedom: A Documentary History of Emancipation*, http://www.freedmen.umd.edu/LL66-67pg.html.

that those who left agricultural employment be arrested and put to work on public roads.[43]

Cecilia joined Wallace on James Island after the birth of her son Robert in 1866, and in early 1867, they moved back to his plantation near Lawtonville, where the baby died of cholera in July. By the end of the year, Wallace sold this property, having decided to return to James Island for good, but he had chosen a particularly inauspicious time to resume planting there. According to the records of the Agricultural Society of South Carolina, "The seasons of 1867 and 1868 were two of the most unfavorable ever known upon the seacoast. Constant rains so saturated the soil as frequently to render the fields impassable to those on horse back, and caterpillars coming in August so completely destroyed the [cotton] crop as to leave...less than twenty pounds per acre for harvest."[44] Cecilia related that her husband was the first to discover the cotton caterpillar in July 1868. After he took one to show to the other James Island planters, he told her that "he never saw men so crestfallen." In September 1868, she wrote that the caterpillars had "stripped the whole fields of cotton of every leaf, leaving only the bare stems."[45]

Cecilia's memoir details the difficult years she and her husband spent on James Island up to late 1872 and includes many excerpts from a diary she "commenced keeping" in 1868. A son, St. John Alison, was born to them in 1869, and a daughter, named Cecilia, came along in 1871. Despite periods of poor health and other setbacks and sorrows, through much hard work and some entrepreneurship, Cecilia and Wallace gradually managed to prosper in a modest way. Wallace started a dairy, and in February 1870, he began supplying milk to the Mills House, a Charleston hotel that would figure largely in the Lawton family's future.

---

[43] Bostick, *Brief History of James Island*, 87.
[44] Agricultural Society of South Carolina Records, Minute book, 1880–1959, 11.
[45] Lawton, "Incidents," 181.

Cecilia's references to certain places in Beaufort District being part of Hampton County indicate that she did not begin writing her memoir until 1878 (when that county was created) or afterward. By this time, her family's improving fortunes must have allowed her time to reflect on the past, and to direct some of her energies toward chronicling an eventful—sometimes tragic—but always interesting life.

Illustrations

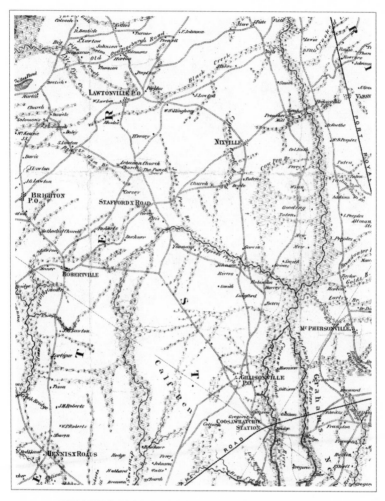

BEAUFORT COUNTY, SOUTH CAROLINA

Detail from an 1870 map of Beaufort County showing the location of
Robertville, Lawtonville, and McPhersonville, all of which were burned
by Federal troops in 1865. The map also shows the location of the
Lawton plantation near Lawtonville. *Courtesy of Library of Congress.*

CECILIA LAWTON

The reverse of this photograph is inscribed: "Cecilia Lawton, aged 22, wife of W. Wallace Lawton, Charleston, S.C. From a photo taken 1870." *Courtesy of Anna Lebby Campbell.*

ANNA LAWTON OSWALD

This photograph of Cecilia's sister Anna Lawton Oswald
dates to the 1890s. *Courtesy of Anna Lebby Campbell.*

ST. JOHN HOTEL

The St. John Hotel in Charleston as it appeared around 1905. Cecilia
Lawton purchased the business in 1901. *Courtesy of Library of Congress.*

Incidents in the Life of

Cecilia Lawton

Cecilia's Story:
Incidents in the Life of Cecilia Lawton

CECILIA, FIFTH DAUGHTER AND eighth child of Robert The-mistocles (Dion) Lawton, and his wife Harriet Charlotte (nee Singellton), was born at the old *Lawton Homestead* in Lawtonville, Beaufort District (afterwards Hampton County), South Carolina, Dec. 11th 1847.[1]

My father and mother were both born near Robertville, Beaufort District, South Carolina, in the section usually called "Black Swamp." They (my parents) were *third cousins*; and both were born in 1807—Papa February 15th and mama Dec. 10th; he being 10 months her senior. They were married Feb. 23rd 1831 at her home as above. Papa's name was originally Robert Themis-tocles *Dion*; the two latter names being for his father, but he dropped the "*Dion*" about the time he was grown deeming his name too long.[2]

The relationship between my parents was through the *Robert* family, Papa's grandmother (Sarah Robert) being a sister of Mama's grandfather (John Robert). They were thus both descend-ants of *Pierre Robert*, the Huguenot minister. This was the only blood relationship between them. Papa's name *Robert* was for his grandmother (Sarah) *Robert*.

Not long before my birth my parents removed from Savan-nah, Ga., where they had taken residence for a good many years, and where my two oldest sisters, Anna and Rosa, grew up. The plantation at Lawtonville was retained by Papa during his sojourn in Savannah.

---

[1] This spelling of the surname "Singellton" is used several times by Cecilia Lawton in this memoir, but the name is most often found in genealogies and other records as "Singleton."

[2] A penciled note follows this paragraph: "Was this originally D'Ion?"

At the time of my birth my parents had only three living children besides, viz, Anna and Rosa, their two oldest, and Georgia, who was nearly 3 years my senior.[3] They had lost four (4) children (three boys and one girl) before the birth of Georgia.

I was always told that I was a remarkably healthy, good-natured baby and child, too fat and rosy to be considered pretty. I never had any illness during my childhood, and a physician was never called in to attend me from my birth until after my marriage, and in consequence of conditions arising therefrom.

My first recollection of impressions received must have been related to as early an age as 18 months, or possibly a few months later, for it was about the time of my being weaned. I was left in charge of my father and a faithful old nurse (Mom Delia) while my mother went on a short trip to the town of Beaufort, where sister Anna (Mrs. Robert Oswald) then resided.[4]

My next remembered impressions were of my brother Aleck, when I was told of his birth and taken in to see him.[5] I was two and a half years old then.

I next recall my delight in being presented with a maid, whom I was told should always be mine—Eleanor, a little negro girl who was a few months my junior. I was not over four years old at the time, and went about the house and yard hand in hand with Eleanor, proclaiming to everyone, "I b'longs to Eleanor!" The

---

[3] The four children were Benjamin Charles Lawton (1835–1844), Thomas Robert Lawton (1842–1844), Willingham Lawton (1838–1839), and Ella Lawton (1840–1841).

[4] Cecilia's sister Anna Lawton (1832–1905) married Robert Oswald (1828–1896), a native of Beaufort, South Carolina. He was the son of Robert Oswald (1793–1834) and Lavinia Chaplin (1803–1868), whose second husband was Hansford Dade Duncan (b. 1787). Among the children of Robert and Anna Oswald were Henry Chovin Oswald (b. 1860); Robert Lawton Oswald (1850–1918); Hansford Dade Oswald (1857–1909); George Douglas Oswald (1863–1938); Rosa Estelle Oswald (1855–1922), who married Croskeys Royall (1855–1941); and Lavinia (Livie) Duncan Oswald (1852–1927), who married John Calhoun Clark (1849–1929). The Oswald plantation was called Jericho.

[5] Cecilia's brother Alexander James Lawton was born in 1850.

laughter this speech produced made a strong impression on me. Eleanor and I were always devoted friends until emancipation separated us. She fell heir to all of my cast-off dresses, and I was ever her champion and defender in domestic trouble with the other slaves or the white children of the family.

During the winter of 1852–53 (in Dec. I think), we moved over to Screven County, Georgia, to a plantation afterwards known as "Blockade Place." A short time before we moved sister Rosa had been married to Walter L. Livingston (Nov. 11th 1852).[6] My mother was sorry to leave her lovely home, whose surroundings she had beautified by many trees and flowers &c, but papa said that he got tired of the constant gossiping and rows of the neighborhood, in which he nor his wife ever took part, though he was invariably appealed to as a judge, or arbitrator. The community had once been very agreeable, but became then unbearable, and so he left it.

My youngest sister, Janie, was born in Screven County, Georgia, when I was about 5½ years old. We lived here for several years, generally returning to S. Carolina during the summer, as our parents at first had misgivings regarding the perfect health of their new home.

My mother never became fully reconciled to living in Screven County. She had no associates, and always wished to move into a more congenial community. Poor, dear heart! Her wish was never gratified.

She did a *great deal* of charity work among her neighbors, being an active, cheerful Christian, but in the nature of events could find no social pleasure in the companionship of unlettered folks. She had been raised in the midst of a charming and refined circle, and was besides quite an heiress for those days, possessing a valuable plantation and many slaves in her own right when she married papa.

---

[6] Walter Livingston (1832–1954) was the son of Philip P. Livingston (1791–1832) of New York and Eliza Barnwell Ashe. Walter and Rosa had one son, Walter, who was born on December 17, 1853, in Screven County, Georgia.

In 1853 Georgia was sent to school in Lawtonville, South Carolina.

When we moved from Lawtonville, sister Anna was living a few miles from there at "Sylvan Home," a place papa had given her, but several years after we moved over to Georgia they returned to Beaufort (S.C.) where her husband had been raised.

When we moved to Screven County, sister Rosa & brother Walter, who had just been married, lived near us for some time, in a small house on papa's place about a mile from our home. Papa and brother Walter had a large steam saw and corn mill erected, but it proved a failure, and the next fall brother Walter returned to Charleston, S.C., followed by sister Rosa as soon as she could travel, for her baby, Walter Chapman, was born in Dec. 1853.[7]

The next summer (1854) the yellow fever raged in Charleston, and sister Rosa and the baby came to us. Brother Walter remained at his business, and took the fever. He recovered sufficiently to join his family, where he had a relapse and died late in the fall of 1854 at our house.

This is my first recollection of *death*. I did not realize that brother Walter's spirit had passed away, and wished that I could have as much attention paid me. I wept, but only because it distressed me to see my mother weeping, and when I found out I could not go to the funeral, I was as much disappointed as if I had missed a juvenile party. I was nearly seven years old.

About this time I was severely punished one day by my father for a supposed falsehood of which I was perfectly innocent, for I was a truthful child. I [bore] no malice, but I never forgot the injustice of it.

Sister Rosa and her baby, Walter, continued to live with us, and after a while, sister Rosa undertook to teach me. Up to this time, I had only been taught by my mother. At seven years of age I was considered very smart because I worked out and understood long examples in Division. I began taking music lessons about the

---

[7] Walter Chapman Livingston died in 1908 and is buried in Philadelphia.

beginning of my eighth year, from Miss Eliza Hobby.[8] I showed quite an aptitude for music. On account of constant moves afterwards, my music lessons and practicing were often interrupted, much to my mother's regret, and my own.

In the fall of 1856 our first governess, Miss Minnie Upson, a Northern lady, was engaged. She went to Albany, Ga. with us, and remained nearly a year. In Nov. or Dec. 1856 we moved to Albany, Ga. This was my first railroad trip, and long had we (the little ones) looked forward to it. We stopped for over a day and night in Macon, Ga., the first city I had ever seen. I and the other children were wild with delight.

Before we moved to Albany, grandmother Lawton (papa's mother), used to pay us long visits in Screven County, having given up her home in South Carolina.[9] She used to come in her own carriage, which she kept always—a handsome [close] carriage, and fine [pair of] bay horses—also her driver, faithful old Monday (son of the African Monday), and her pretty mulatto maid Nellie, whom I used to love dearly. Grandmother was a lovely old lady, immaculate in dress as in conversation. She died while we were in Albany, Ga. (spring of 1857).

After reaching Albany, we lived for several years in a new and roomy cottage in the main street of the town (Broad St.) near the river (Flint River). Then we moved to a house in the suburbs which papa had bought. It had about two acres of ground attached to it, for gardens, orchards, &c.

Papa here erected a school house on one corner of his lot and generously allowed Miss Upson (whose whole time he had engaged) to take other select scholars and thus increase her income.

Papa had been persuaded to go to Albany by "uncle Joe" (Col W. J. Lawton), who had moved to that section several years

---

[8] This was likely Eliza Hobby (1829–1911), a teacher and artist, and the daughter of William Johnston Hobby (1805–1840).

[9] Cecilia's paternal grandmother was Jane Mosse Lawton (1783–1857), the widow of Benjamin Themistocles Dion Lawton (1782–1846).

before.[10] Papa and uncle Joe were engaged in building a railroad from Americus to Albany. I believe they built all of it, which was then called the South Western Rail Road.[11] On our way to Albany, we had to stage it from Americus.

Very soon after our arrival in Albany, sister Rosa met Dr. George Baskerville Douglas, and they have always said that it was a case of "love at first sight."[12] She was a *very* youthful widow, and he a handsome, well-preserved widower of nearly forty. Dr. Douglas had an only son by his first wife. This boy (George Craighead) was then twelve years of age. He came to spend Christmas with his father, and I shall ever recall with amusement the evening his father took him to our new home to make his first call—the anxiety of his father that his boy should make a good impression on his lady-love, and George's natural, happy, unrestrained manner. His cheeks were round and very rosy, and he was the picture of health. Poor fellow! He died in the prime of life, a victim to the barbarities undergone in a Yankee prison while a prisoner of war. His mother was a sister of Gov. Ellis of North Carolina.

Sister Rosa (widow of Walter Livingston) was married to Dr. George B. Douglas at our home in Albany, Ga. Nov. 31st 1857, which was Georgia's 12th birthday, and she was therefore permitted to be one of the bride's attendants.

I shall remember with pleasure that evening all my days. We were kindly allowed to invite several of our family friends to be present, but the first guest to arrive was an unexpected one. George Douglas ran away from boarding-school and came to his

---

[10] Winborn Joseph Lawton (1817–1884) was a planter in Dougherty County, Georgia, and a railroad builder.

[11] The South Western Railroad was chartered in 1845. In 1857 it bought a smaller railroad company, the Georgia and Florida, which had been building a line from Americus to Albany, and undertook to finish the route.

[12] George Baskerville Douglas (1816–1899) was a native of Virginia. He studied medicine at the University of Pennsylvania and first practiced in Salisbury, North Carolina, where he met his first wife, Mary Ellis, the sister of John Willis Ellis (1820–1861), who was elected governor of North Carolina in 1859.

father's wedding, and under the circumstances, was readily forgiven. His bright explanations and excuses and merry laughter kept a circle of amused friends about him all the evening.

Papa had intended settling permanently in Albany, and mama was also anxious for it, as we there had the advantage of church, society, &c, but when she found that fever and ague prevailed throughout the county in summer, she was unwilling to remain.

Our plantation in Screven County had been carried on, as only the youngest of the negroes had been taken off to work on the railroad, and in July (?) we returned there, but did not remain for the summer, going over to stay with sister Anna near Lawtonville, South Carolina until fall.

Papa took us to Screven and then returned to Albany, being still engaged in the railroad there. He was also president of a bank, the only one in Albany.

On our way from Albany, when near Macon, the train came near plunging into a washout caused by heavy rain, and we had to sleep all night in the train eating only cold food of which, however, mama had such a generous supply, that she fed all the passengers. The next morning early stages and carriages arrived and took us on a roundabout road to Macon. All of this proved a great frolic to us.

Mama had been very ill in Albany the first part of the year, with Typhoid pneumonia I think, and Dr. Douglas attended her (and paid addresses to sister Rosa at the same time).

We never returned to Albany. The family had only lived there about 8 months, but papa had been there working on the railroad for 6 months or more before we went, and continued until the close of 1857, when *his* contract was completed. During this time he paid constant visits to Screven.

Sister Anna & brother Robert moved back to Beaufort during the winter of 1857–1858.

Early in 1858 papa took the youngest and most robust of his negroes, and went out to Pierce County, Ga., where he engaged in work on the Savannah, Albany and Gulf R.R., usually called the "Gulf Road."[13]

His first settlement was near a station called "Zero" on the Satilla River. Zero was the then terminus of the R.R. He lived at first in a tent, having gone well provided with such. But he soon erected log cabins for himself & his slaves, and after a while my mother joined him, her wifely devotion overcoming her anxiety lest she should find his temporary home in the woods too uncomfortable. He tried to persuade her to remain in Savannah where he could visit us every week. We called our camping place "The Shanties" and we (the children) enjoyed the new life vastly. We thought the large log house with its wide clay chimney the ideal home. The country was wild and uncivilized, *much* more so than Screven County.

We took our own trained house servants with us, and furniture enough to make us comfortable. But the only visitors we ever had were the young men in the surveying corps, of whom I remember Mr. Law and Mr. Maxwell. They were glad to have a congenial family to visit, and my parents enjoyed their conversation. Even now I recall overhearing mama giving motherly counsel to one of them who was inclined to be wild.

Connected with papa in this railroad building was a Mr. Lundy of Albany, Georgia, and his (papa's) brother, our uncle Capt. Alexander B. Lawton of Florida.[14] The latter lived with his family just across the railroad track from us, in quite a pretentious "shanty" for that region. Uncle Aleck brought with him his children's tutor, Mr. Robert L. Baker, a young man just graduated

---

[13] The Savannah, Albany and Gulf Railroad was chartered in 1847 (as the Savannah and Albany Railroad) to build a rail connection from the southwest region of Georgia to the port of Savannah, but the company was not fully organized until about 1853. By May 1859, its line reached the town of Blackshear in Pierce County.

[14] Alexander Benjamin Lawton (1809–1861) owned Summer Oaks, a plantation in Thomas County, Georgia. His wife was Narcissa Melissa Lawton (1817–1883).

from Oglethorpe College, Ga. Mr. Baker taught us also, my sister Georgia ("Dauda" was her nickname), my small brother Aleck and myself, also uncle Aleck's three boys (Winnie, Robert & Tommy) and daughter Clara.[15] The eldest son, Robert, was off at college. A small school house was erected halfway between uncle Aleck's house and ours, and here we attended school for several months.

It was through a window of this school house that one day we saw our little sister Janie in a blaze. Dauda (Georgia) saw her first, and ran out of the school house, I following her. When we reached the spot, Janie was being borne into the house by a servant, my mother following, wringing her hands. There was scarcely a shred of clothing left on poor Janie, and the skin hung like rags from one arm. Her beautiful, long brown curls were burnt off close to her head. The poor little darling lived about seven or eight weeks after being burned, and died of dropsy and other complications, June 24th 1858.

Some of the wounds had not entirely healed when she died. She was five (5) years & 25 days old. I was at that time ten years old, and distinctly recall my mother's grief, and my own as well. Darling mama nursed her "baby" day and night, knowing no rest, and when her pure spirit took its flight, she broke down, and was an invalid for months. She seemed to have lost all interest in life. It was principally on account of her depressed condition that papa planned the camping expedition in the fall, described later on.

While we were at the first "Shanty" near here, sister Rosa and brother George (Dr. & Mrs. Douglas) arrived very unexpectedly, bringing their very young infant, a few weeks old, to show to its grandparents. She had been named "Harriet Singellton" for my mother, and was born January 1858. I remember my mother's horror at the child being brought to such an open house in cold weather. But we were all delighted to see them, and they enjoyed

---

[15] These were Winborn Theodore Lawton (1843–1892), Robert W. Lawton (b. 1847), Thomas J. Lawton (b. 1851), and Clara J. Lawton (b. 1845).

the novel surroundings of our temporary abode. Little Walter Livingston (sister Rosa's son by first marriage) also came with them.

A few days after Janie's death, we moved about four miles farther up the railroad tracks, as that portion of the road bed had been completed. These were "Shanties No. 2." Here little Janie's body was buried in our enclosed garden quite near the house. It was never removed, though papa often promised mama to do so, and she grieved much over the neglect.

Some years later a man from Screven County (name forgotten) moved to this place and settled. But as the land belonged to the state (Georgia), & papa had been the first settler, the man was obliged to get titles from papa before he could legally claim the land. Papa gave him the necessary papers upon condition that he would always protect and care for Janie's grave.

Mama continued in such poor health after little Janie's death that in the fall (Sept. or Oct.) papa proposed to take us back home (Screven County) by private conveyance through the country, camping out at night. We had previously stopped school, as papa did not like Mr. Baker's management.

There were reports of yellow fever in Savannah so we gave that place a wide berth, selecting a healthy, pineland country to travel through. We camped out at night in a very large comfortable tent, had our own cooks and provisions, and *thoroughly enjoyed* the trip. The weather was delightful, and by the time we arrived home mama's health was much improved, and she seemed to take a fresh interest in life.

We must have been about 6 days on the trip. We had a large covered wagon, a cart, & our family conveyance besides. As the country we traversed was settled only by the poorest farmers, we were more comfortable in our camp than we should have been in their houses.

In September 1858, a very short time before our camping expedition, there was a violent equinoctial gale which came near demolishing our shanty home. A *very* large pine tree was rooted up in our yard and hurled across the roof of our house, crashing into us, and falling over our bed, almost touching it, for "Dauda" & I roomed upstairs. The rain poured in upon my mother, who was sick in bed, her room being just under ours. Papa wrapped her in a large cloak and bore her in his arms into Mary's house (our family nurse, "Mara"). She was a large woman but his great strength was equal to the burden.

Mr. Wm. ("Billy") Bee of Savannah came to live with us some time before we left "Shanty No. 2." He assisted papa with his accounts &c, but papa gave him a home more out of personal interest than for other consideration. He knew his family and liked him personally, & tried to influence him for good. I was a great favorite with "Billy Bee" and he predicted that I would grow up *a beauty*.

After our return to Screven County, Georgia went to Beaufort to visit sister Anna and Robbie Oswald remained with us.

1859. At the opening of this year, we were living on our plantation in Screven County, Georgia, though papa was still working on the "Gulf" Railroad in Southern Ga. About March we left the plantation. Papa took me to Beaufort, S.C. intending to enter me there at school where "Dauda" (sister Georgia) was, but finding her eyes quite bad, he changed his plans, and took us both back with him.

In Savannah at the Screven House we met mama and "the boys," Aleck and Robbie Oswald, and after remaining long enough to consult Dr. Bullock about Dauda's eyes, we all proceeded to Clinch County where papa's railroad work was.[16] The trip to Beaufort, South Carolina, was a delightful one. I took my first sea voyage going there (on Steamer Cecile) and my first view of salt water.

---

[16] At this time the Atlantic and Gulf Railroad, chartered in 1856, was being built through Clinch County, Georgia. It was built "in a southwestern direction through territory rich in resources and which had never been opened up. The road was completed to Homerville in the fall of 1859" (Huxford, *History of Clinch County*, 44).

Sister Anna was living at her husband's ancestral home "Jerico" on the Broad River, a few miles from the town. We spent several days there, and wading in the salt water, picking up shells, &c were new & charming pleasures to me. I was a well-grown girl of 11 years, but quite a romp.

Arriving at the terminus of the railroad, we had a distance of sixty miles to travel before reaching *Shanties No. 3* in Clinch County. All intervening streams were much swollen by recent floods of rain, and we were compelled to remain at the terminus for a long time, probably ten days, hoping each day to leave.

We were taken in by young married couple from southwest Georgia (named Austin), who treated us with every consideration and kindness, but they had lately arrived themselves and their house was small.[17] One night papa and the boys had to sleep on some hay in their barn, for mama and the girls had the only available bedroom, and quite a small one.

As soon as the streams became passable, we traveled on to *Shanty No. 3*, about 8 or 10 miles from Magnolia, the county seat of Clinch or Ware County?[18]

We had a magnificent pair of bays (Prince & Albert) that papa had recently purchased, & our carriage, which had been built for travelling, and a one horse buggy besides. Also a wagon with baggage. We stopped one night at a farm house which looked large and new and clean, but the bed linen was so uncleanly that Mama sent out to the wagon and had some of her own bed clothes unpacked. Also borrowed several new patchwork quilts from the farmer's wife, which were kept as *ornaments* on a set of shelves in the parlor.

---

[17] This was likely William M. Austin (1830–1912), who "at various times was in the employment of the Atlantic & Gulf Railroad." His wife was Harriet E. Austin (Ibid., 223).

[18] The words "Clinch or Ware Co.?" were penciled in at the end of this sentence. Now extinct, Magnolia, originally called Polk, was a small village in Clinch County, Georgia. The nearby town of Homerville replaced it as the county seat of Clinch County in 1860.

My mother was haunted by fears of a skin disease (which shall be nameless) said to abound in that country & which attacks one's hands especially.

When we were seated at the table in this house, our heads only could be seen across the table, the latter being very high, and the homemade chairs *very low*. Our supper consisted of an immense dish of *fried bacon* swimming in grease, and a very large dish of *corn dodgers*, or hot cakes, supplemented by Rio coffee minus sugar or milk. Needless to add that we retired hungry to our room and hunted up our lunch basket.

"Shanty No. 3" was situated in a pretty grove of pine trees near the stage road. Twice a week we would hear the stage horn and run to the front door to see the stagecoach pass with its four horses and its flourish of trumpet, and then a negro boy would run out and climb up a pine tree and bring us our mail, for papa had a box nailed to a tree just in front of our house, and it was just at a convenient height for the stage driver seated on his high box to reach. This was how we received and sent off our mail.

While at this place sister Rosa paid us a visit, bringing her two children, Walter and Hattie, also George Douglas, her husband's son by his first marriage. They lived still in Albany, Georgia, where her husband had a *very large* practice.

Sister Rosa had been with us several weeks when we left for the North. We had quite an exciting time in reaching the train in time, as the stagecoach failed us. Previous to this, however, papa had taken Aleck and Robbie to Beaufort, S.C., where they were put to school, for sister Anna was then living in the town.

In July (or perhaps Aug. 1st) papa, sister Rosa, Dauda (sister Georgia) and I left for the North *via* Savannah, where we remained several days before sailing at the Pulaski House. We sailed for Philadelphia on Steamer "State of Georgia," & I had my first case of *mal de mere* before Tybee Island was passed.

George Douglas, Walter (Livingston) and Hattie were left with mama, who also gave general directions in papa's absence, wrote him accounts of business &c during his absence. Mama did not care of traveling. (What a helpmate she was! And how many noble and useful and lovely traits were combined in her!) Mr. Billy Bee also remained to assist with the business (I think).

We remained several days in Philadelphia at the grandest hotel I had ever seen (the Gerard, I think). We did a good deal of sight seeing. I recall most vividly Independence Hall, with its bell in the tower, Fairmont Park, and the trip up the Schuykill River, where the view enchanted my eyes.

I also recall my wild delight on seeing the tiny steamboats along the Delaware Bay and the river on our approaching Philadelphia. They seemed to me like little toy boats made for children.

In Philadelphia papa had Georgia's and my pictures taken. I was thin, very thin, that summer, for the first time in my life. Mama feared malaria, & so consented to my going North, young as I was.

From Philadelphia we went to Bethlehem, Pennsylvania, where we were left at the Bethlehem Female Seminary, and papa and sister Rosa after remaining a few days, continued their travels. This was a Moravian school, and the principal was Rev. Sylvester Wolle. Rev. Francis Wolle, his brother, being the vice-president.[19]

It was vacation when we arrived, but a good many girls were there as summer boarders. I was eleven years old, and my sister Georgia was fourteen.

Papa & sister Rosa took quite an extensive trip through the North and Canada, returning in September, after school began, to see us before going South. At Elmira, New York, papa broke his arm by jumping from a carriage as the horses were dashing furiously towards the river, & no driver.

1859 & 1860. As winter advanced Dauda's eyes began troubling her again. In November she went to Newark New Jersey in charge of Mr. Wolle's widowed sister (whom papa of course paid),

---

[19] Rev. Sylvester Wolle (1816–1873), a native of Jacobsburg, Pennsylvania, was in charge of the Bethlehem Female Seminary from 1849 to 1861. His brother was Francis Henry Augustus Wolle (1817–1893). The seminary was founded in 1785.

and Dr. Clark, the celebrated oculist, treated her eyes.[20] But neither her eyes or her health improved. The Northern winter was too severe for her, and so about Feb. 1st, she left Bethlehem and returned home, leaving me at school.

In the meantime papa had returned to Screven with all his slaves, and gave up railroad building permanently. Indeed, he promised his slaves never to engage in it again, for they were not as comfortable as when at their houses, where they all had their crops, chickens, pigs and some cows. Besides this the slave-negro *disliked extremely* to change his abode. Like the cat, he had strong local attachments.[21]

Upon my sister Georgia's return from Bethlehem, Pa., mama began fretting about my being there alone, young as I was, and papa wrote for me to go home by the Steamer "State of Georgia" in care of the captain (Garvin), an old acquaintance of his. Papa could not leave home at the time, and Dauda (Georgia) had returned safely in the same way, papa meeting her in Savannah. Accordingly I was taken to Philadelphia (in March, I think) by old Mr. (Rev.) Francis Wolle, our vice-principal, to meet the Savannah steamer.

A small middle-aged Indian woman accompanied us to Philadelphia.[22] Her history had been peculiar. Her Indian father had been a chief and a very wealthy land owner. He put his little girl at Mr. Wolle's school to be educated. But he died soon after, and the child had been abandoned by her relatives and her property unlawfully held by a wicked white brother-in-law. After several

---

[20] This was Dr. James Henry Clark (1814–1869).

[21] John T. Trowbridge, a northern newspaperman who toured the South after the war, made a similar observation about the freedmen, noting the "almost religious attachment of these people to their homes" (Trowbridge, *The South*, 544).

[22] The Moravians had been operating missions and schools for several Native American tribes since the latter part of the eighteenth century, which may explain the presence of the "Indian woman." In the nineteenth century, the Moravians had missions in Kansas and elsewhere, and in Kansas worked with the Chippewa and Munsee peoples.

years, having given up hope of receiving funds for the abandoned child, and there being no provision at the school for such children, kind Mr. Francis Wolle received the little girl into his house, where she grew up a "help" in household work, but also as a member of the family. His daughters (all younger than the Indian waif) seemed devotedly attached to her, and followed her to the R.R. station, parting with affection & regrets. The wicked brother-in-law had at last discovered a conscience, and had sent for the woman to restore her rights to her. She was a neat-looking little woman yet I recall my abhorrence of sleeping with her because of her race, though I was a timid child, and frightened to death at sleeping alone in the big hotel. I had a bed in the room with her, but terror at length made me creep to her bed, which she kindly asked me to share.

We remained two days in Philadelphia, but our steamer did not arrive, having stuck on a bank at mouth of Savannah River. Mr. Wolle took me back to the school in Bethlehem, and after a week or more of suspense, it was finally determined that I should remain until end of term, when papa could come for me. Also my studies had been much interrupted, and I wept bitterly at the disappointment when I found I was not to go home.

The plan upon which the Bethlehem Female Seminary was conducted was peculiar. The girls were divided into companies or "Rooms" as they were called, ranging from the 9th to the 1st room, according to age, and one extra room called the "German Room," where only that language was spoken and presided over by a lady teacher imported from Germany for the purpose. There were about 20 or more girls in each room. I was not allowed to be in the room with my sister, as she was about 3 years older, & their rules were inflexible. So I was put into "Room No. 9," being among the youngest of the scholars. I studied French and music as extras to the regular course. My French teacher (a Frenchman by birth & education) told me that I acquired the pronunciation so readily, he knew that I had French blood in me. I was a favorite with him, & the youngest girl in the class.

We had a large and quite a pretty playground at the school, enjoying drifting down the long hill on our little sleds in winter when it was covered with snow, and swinging and spinning round on the merry-go-round in summer. In pleasant weather, we took long walks every day. In summer & spring we were taken on picnics every now and then, generally to a pretty wooded island in the Monocacy or Lehigh River, or on the mountain side. In winter we enjoyed occasional sleigh rides, a new delight to southern girls.

Bethlehem was a pretty & quaint little mountain town, & quite old & of German origin. It is situated in the Lehigh Valley in the midst of the coal region. The school was founded by Moravians, and was very old also. The main building was *heavily* built of stone & had been used in the Revolutionary War as a hospital. Tradition said that General [?] had been taken wounded into it, and some of my schoolmates, knowing I was a timid little girl, informed me that the dark spots on the floor of our dormitory, directly under my bed, had been made by his blood.

One of the superstitions of the place was that these spots could never be washed out, and that the ghost of the old hero lingered about them still. The story sufficed to cause me nights of *terror* unspeakable. For hours I would lay covered up head & ears & trembling with superstitious awe, too terrified to sleep. As a child I had a very vivid imagination, which portrayed all manner of unreal & unheard of forms and performances to harrow my soul. Until some years later I was a firm believer in ghostly visitants, & in all the superstitions of the slave negroes, whose stories had a fearful fascination for my youthful mind. I did not doubt for a moment that the skeletons of the dead frequently sprang from their graves and pursued the living. I believed implicitly all such stories told me by my negro nurses & our slaves generally.

When school closed for the summer vacation, I remained with about 15 or 20 other girls as boarders under the care of Rev. Dr. Wolle and one lady teacher, as papa could not come on immediately. He wrote word that he would bring my sister Georgia on and take us with him for an extensive trip through the

Northern states & Canada. But being dreadfully home-sick, I begged him to take me home instead. Thus I lost a delightful trip, which I have always regretted.

During vacation, rules being relaxed, I was robbed of nearly my whole wardrobe including ribbon, sashes (which were handsome & abundant) and jewelry. I was only 12 years old & did not know how to guard my belongings.

I recall that the Philadelphia National Guards, considered a very fine company of gentlemen, came over to Bethlehem on an encampment, & that Mr. Wolle, our principal, gave them a fine dinner (4th of July) spread on a long table under the trees on our playground.[23] The girls all helped to serve them with food, and I recall my father's disgust when he heard how his daughter had been employed, for party feeling ran very high, and there were already mutterings of war in the land.

During the time we were at this school in Bethlehem, Pennsylvania (Oct. 16th or 17th) occurred the riot at Harper's Ferry, Va., led by John Brown, abolitionist, who incited the negroes to rise against their masters. The report flew through the North that all the slaves in the South had been freed, and some dozen Northern girls undertook to bear this startling news to all the Southern girls in the school and to exult over them. I recall how they came bearing down upon me, a little child of 11 years. But their manners were so rude & insolent that though I was taken by surprise, my pride rose to the occasion. I cooly informed them that we had other property besides slaves, and that my father could support his family under any circumstances. They got no satisfaction & left me in supreme disgust.

I heard that they had caused one Southern girl to burst into tears. They attributed her grief to the supposed loss of property, when she, being old enough to understand the horrors of an insurrection, was doubtless alarmed for the safety of her family.

---

[23] This was a state militia organization.

At school here my closest friends were Sallie Cairns of Memphis, Tennessee (her father was the General Cairns of Confederate War) and Katie Knoll, a pretty girl of German descent from Philadelphia.[24] They were both good, studious girls, & about my age.

I also felt deeply interested in Ellie [Torbert], a little motherless half-breed from Maine, Sandwich Islands. Her father was a Quaker from Philadelphia, her mother an Indian of Sandwich Islands, where Ellie was born. The Yankee girls persecuted poor little Ellie because she was alone & thousands of miles from her home, as they did a California girl, who was a very nice little girl. I felt for them both.

There were nearly 250 girls in this school. Each "Room" or company (20 or more) had its own study & classroom, dressing room, bathroom & dormitory, also own table. We were always guarded by a lady teacher & were not allowed to talk except at play time. We became very expert at signs, finger alphabet, &c.

I remember our "May Party" in Bethlehem. Our "Room" had a very nice picnic-party at [Naski] Hill, a public park on the hillside overlooking the river. May [Kapper] of Va. was our queen, Aggie Walter of Washington, D.C., her child maid of honor. I was also one of the six maids of honor. I had a beautiful dress to wear, but being easily cajoled, a *very horrid* German girl persuaded me to exchange with her, & thus I appeared at the picnic in a very common dress that was much too short and narrow, while the unscrupulous roommate wore my handsome dress, which she tore to shreds climbing trees, so that I could never wear it again.

The above shows one of my weak, if kindly, traits. At that time, I was often imposed upon. *But on the whole I had a happy time.*

---

[24] James Alexander Carnes (1808–1864), a Memphis merchant, held the rank of brigadier general in the Tennessee militia. In 1862, "a Memphis newspaper reported that his brigade was ordered into service to protect that city" (Allardice, *More Generals in Gray*, 245). He had a daughter named Sally Little Carnes (1848–1885).

The girl above referred to was a fraud and an adventuress. She was very much older than she claimed, & being thus roomed with younger girls, made use of us to suit herself. That such as she was are sometimes admitted into boarding schools, has ever been with me a strong reason against sending young girls to boarding schools to be made dupes or led into evil ways.

1860. Papa came for me in July. I was so overjoyed at seeing him that I burst into floods of hysterical weeping and clung to him. It was a good long time before I could control myself, an hour or more. I was very much surprised at myself when I afterwards recalled what an exhibition I had made of myself before everyone.

I was so very fat at this time, that papa said he scarcely recognized me. We were fed *five times a day*, German style, on plain food.

Papa wished to take me over to New York to see the "Great Eastern," the largest ship ever built. It was on exhibition in New York. But I wanted to start at once for home, & so missed it. This huge steamship proved a failure as an ocean passenger boat, as was designed, but afterwards it came into use in laying ocean cables, there being abundant room for the coils of wire &c.

Papa took me home via Baltimore, Chesapeake Bay, by steamer Norfolk, and from thence by rail via Augusta. Everything looked so changed to me at home that I felt out of place at first. In fact, nothing was changed, but my surroundings, methods of life &c, had been so very different, and 12 months is a long period in a child's life.

I had grown so tall and *stout* that Eleanor, my beloved little maid, refused to believe it was her little mistress and would not greet me. At this I burst into tears.

Dauda (sister Georgia) went, soon after my return from Bethlehem, on a visit to sister Anna at Beaufort, South Carolina. She remained until fall, when she went to Orangeburg Female College, South Carolina. It was kept by Rev. I. S. Keith Legare, a

Presbyterian minister.[25] Nearly all the girls were from South Carolina.

We had never attended the schools in Screven County, our parents being exclusive, and fearing that we would get what they termed the "Cracker twang" in speaking. But at this time there was an excellent Academy at Bascom 4 miles from our home, kept by a gentleman & his wife who were recently from Massachusetts, Dr. & Mrs. Bridgman. He was a brother of Laura Bridgman, the famous blind deaf-mute, who has been so much written of.[26]

I was wild to remain at home, and continued begging and pleading with my parents until they permitted me to have my way instead of going to Orangeburg with Dauda. Therefore Aleck and I entered the Bascom Academy in the early fall, driving there & back every day in a one horse buggy. Dr. & Mrs. Bridgman were excellent teachers, & took a special interest in us. Mama had been kind to the young Northern bride, who found her surroundings in that rough country place anything but congenial. And, for her part, Mrs. Bridgman continued a firm and devoted friend to mama until the latter's death in 1863.

It was while at this school that I met and learned to appreciate Fanny Sharpe, the pretty daughter of a widow who lived near us.[27] She was the only friend & companion of my age that I had in the country, or was permitted to have. Our parents kept us strictly aloof from our neighbors.

During the fall the South was in a ferment, & party feeling ran high. The South was almost unanimous in declaring for secession when it was found that Lincoln & Hamlin had been voted in

---

[25] This was Reverend Isaac Stockton Keith Legare (1809–1874).

[26] Dr. Addison Daniel Bridgman (1832–1916), a native of Massachusetts, married Salome Sprague (1835–1911) on August 21, 1860. His sister was Laura Dewey Lynn Bridgman (1829–1889), who was left blinded and deaf from scarlet fever at the age of two. Charles Dickens wrote about her in his *American Notes*.

[27] This was probably Frances Caroline Sharpe (b. 1848), the daughter of Green Duke Sharpe (1823–1858), a Screven County planter and timber man. His widow was Ann Elizabeth Zeigler Sharpe (1827–1901).

as president & vice president, knowing their views on slavery & states rights. But for the greater part the inhabitants of Screven County took a lukewarm interest in the popular movement. There were few educated men among them, & very few large slave owners.

My father was an exception to their rules, & was eager for secession, having always been an adherent of John C. Calhoun's views on this matter. I remember one morning going to school with a "palmetto" or secession cockade pinned on my left front. It was a blue rosette of ribbon with two pieces of palmetto crossed in the middle. Dauda had sent us several from Orangeburg. As I marched in, Dr. Bridgman, spying the cockade, asked me what it was. I informed him. He looked much disgusted, and made some sarcastic remark about the secession movement, for he was a Yankee & had recently come South.

N.B. A year after that he went into the Confederate Army, fought through the war, and came out a *strong Southerner* in feelings.

While I was at this school Mrs. Bridgman taught me Arithmetic by myself. She was a good mathematician herself, and thought I had a wonderful mathematical mind. She said that one example which I worked out unaided (in partial fragments, I think) had never been understood or worked out before by any scholar she had taught during a period of ten years. She got me to explain the example, & was convinced that I understood it. She then took it to a young college graduate in the village who, after working on it for 2 days, gave it up. Mrs. Bridgman was very proud of her little 12 year old mathematician after this.

About this time papa began planning to build a new dwelling in his Screven County Home Place. The lumber was selected with great care from his own saw mill, and the house was well-built & large, having 14 rooms (most of them 20 x 20), 12 fireplaces, large halls up & down stairs, and long piazza back & front. But before it could be completed as he wished, the blockade of our ports compelled him to leave it as it was. Materials needed for the finishing could not be obtained. This caused us to call the new dwelling "Blockade House." At first it was called this as a joke, but finally the place came to be known only as "Blockade Place."

We moved into "Blockade House" in the spring of 1862, as the old house was too small for our large family—parents, children & grandchildren, with our teacher. Papa decided to leave the finishing until the war closed.

It was the custom for sisters Anna & Rosa, with their families, to spend the month of December with us at our home in Screven County. Papa would [bark] his sugar cane and keep it until they arrived, as the children enjoyed seeing the grinding & boiling. It was a great frolic for us, & we never tired of watching the process & of drinking the sweet juice of the cane, & eating the delightful fresh syrup.

Papa's place was a cotton plantation, but he made enough syrup, rice, corn &c for our use and that of his slaves.

1860. I was on a visit to relatives in Lawtonville, South Carolina, having gone there in private conveyance (across the Savannah River) with sisters Anna & Rosa, and we were at Aunt Phoebe Willingham's *beautiful* home when South Carolina seceded from the Union.[28]

December 20th 1860 the convention assembled at Charleston, adopted the ordinance of secession. There was wild excitement, & companies began to be formed. They were called "Minute Men," meaning they were ready to go forth at a minute's notice.[29]

---

[28] This was Phoebe Sarah Lawton Willingham (1808–1862), the daughter of Benjamin Themistocles Dion Lawton (1782–1846). She was the wife of Thomas Henry Willingham (1798–1873).

[29] The "Minute Men" formed in response to the possibility of war, and also in reaction to the "Wide Awakes," a paramilitary organization that formed in the North in the late 1850s and became closely affiliated with the Republican Party and the presidential election of 1860. The Wide Awakes marched in the streets of Northern cities with torches and drilled in uniform as if preparing for military action. Historian Jon Grinspan noted that their militarism "sent an ominous message to those already apprehensive about the Republican party's antisouthern attitudes" ("Young Men for War," 358).

There was a *large house party* at Aunt Phoebe's and many young people and children. We had music, charades, and other games, & a real jolly time. Some of us (the children) were comparing travels, & very few of us could claim to have been outside of the United States. But a smart young man who had been an amused listener suddenly exclaimed, "Why you are all outside of the United States now!"

On my return to my home in Georgia I addressed a letter to one of my cousins "Independent Republic of South Carolina" in bold characters.

Dauda had returned home for the Xmas vacation, and in the early part of 1861, probably already wearied of the Bascom Academy which I had been so anxious to enter, & was glad to go. Dauda would have me enter the Sophomore Class with her, although I now think it would have been better had I entered a class lower. I was just 12 years old.

January 19th 1861 the Georgia convention assembled at Milledgeville (the then capital), passed the ordinance of secession. Papa was not a member (he always avoided [being] dragged into politics as office holder), but he was so deeply interested that he went up to Milledgeville & attended the convention. *His brother, W. J. Lawton* (Uncle Joe) was one of the delegates & therefore a signer of the ordinance. At that time uncle Joe lived in Albany, Ga. & was a wealthy planter & ex-lawyer. He was afterwards *colonel* in the Confederate Army.[30]

During the time I was at Orangeburg Female College momentous events occurred—momentous and exciting at the time—but vastly more momentous in their final results than we imagined. The States of the South were seceding one by one, forts,

---

[30] Winborn Joseph Lawton became colonel of the 2nd Georgia Cavalry Regiment in May 1862, but he was not a signer of the Georgia Ordinance of Secession. Cecilia's cousin Benjamin William Lawton (1822–1879), a physician, was a signer of the South Carolina Ordinance of Secession and lived in Georgia after the war. Dr. Lawton's house in Allendale was burned by Sherman's troops because he signed the ordinance.

arsenals & other property of the Federal government was being captured & held in Southern cities, government officials from the South, members of the president's cabinet, senators & congressmen, army & navy men, were resigning their positions under the U.S. government & hastening to offer their services to their native states in their forthcoming struggle for freedom.

February 4th 1861, Confederate government formed at Montgomery, Alabama. April 13th 1861, the Confederate troops under Gen. G. T. Beauregard bombarded Fort Sumter in Charleston Harbor & captured it from Maj. Anderson the U.S. officer in command.[31]

In anticipation of this event, troops were sent from all points to Charleston, & daily long trains loaded with volunteers passed through Orangeburg. In the afternoons we were permitted to go down the front paling of our grounds & see them pass, for the trains all stopped within a stone's throw of our grounds.

Both of my brothers-in-law joined the army early in 1861. Brother George was made surgeon of 1st Georgia Regiment or Battalion, and afterwards transferred to the Confederate Army when the Southern States had formed their government.[32] This was Dr. Douglas. Brother Robert (Oswald) joined the Beaufort Artillery April 13th or 14th & later entered Kirk's Cavalry.[33]

N.B. Both of them served during the *entire war*, Brother George (Dr. George Baskerville Douglas) as surgeon-major, and brother Robert (Oswald) as sergeant.

When school closed about the last of June, I went home by private conveyance, via Allendale, Barnwell County, where mama

---

[31] The bombardment of Fort Sumter began on April 12, 1861, and ended the next day.

[32] Dr. George Baskerville Douglas first served as assistant surgeon of the 1st Georgia Regiment and then as surgeon of the 6th Georgia Brigade. He was later assigned to organizing and managing military hospitals in Virginia and Georgia.

[33] The 19th Battalion, South Carolina Cavalry, also known as Kirk's Battalion, was formed in December 1864 and included a company called Kirk's Squadron Partisan Rangers.

was on a visit to Uncle Stoney's family (Dr. James Stoney Lawton). Uncle Stoney lived in luxurious style & in a large & very handsome house surrounded by lovely gardens & trees.[34]

Dauda's health failed again, and in May (I think) she went home, papa coming for her. Her eyes gave her so much trouble that she could not study. Thus, for a second time she had to leave me at boarding school.

In the fall of 1861 papa made an arrangement with Mrs. Bridgman to live with us and teach us. She had been married only one year, and her husband (Dr. Addison D. Bridgman) had been persecuted by some of the rowdies in the neighborhood (Screven County was full of such) until he decided to join the army. These men though not in service themselves, insisted that he, a stranger and Northerner, should go forth to fight their country's battles. They called him an enemy to the South, and said they would mob him if he did not.

Papa saw the injustice of their demands, condemned their lawless behavior, and sympathized deeply with Dr. Bridgman and his young wife. But the rowdy element in the community was *too* strong for one upright and honorable gentleman, however much respected, to keep in check. Papa first moved Dr. & Mrs. Bridgman to one of his plantations adjoining ours, where there was a neat, comfortable house, and afterwards, when Dr. Bridgman was forced to enter the army by their inhuman threats, he took Mrs. Bridgman to our house, and promised to protect her and give her a home as long as she needed one. But she was by no means dependent upon us for her support. She was a splendid teacher and we were fortunate to have her with us. In all branches except the languages and music she was *par excellence*.

I remember the afternoon that papa brought her to our house. She had just parted with her husband, not knowing when she would see him again, or if he would be killed in the war, and she was weeping bitterly. Mama, always kindhearted and

---

[34] This was Dr. James Stoney Lawton (1821–1891).

sympathetic, took her at once into her own room, put her arms about her, and soothed her in her own sweet, motherly way, leaving in the parlor the visitors she had been entertaining.

As soon as Mrs. Bridgman came to us, several of the well-to-do neighbors begged papa to allow her to teach their children also. He kindly consented for her to take a few only of them *subject to his approval*. This arrangement increased her income. We went to school at "The Mill" for a while and afterwards in a small schoolhouse that papa erected at the head of our avenue. I recall how strict papa was regarding our associating with even these few selected scholars of Mrs. Bridgman's, insisting that we (the girls) should walk to the school with Mrs. Bridgman & return with her, and after nearly two years had elapsed, in riding past one day near the schoolhouse, he thought he saw me playing near the schoolhouse with the other children, and removed me from Mrs. Bridgman's school that afternoon (Spring of 1863).

He had made a mistake as the girl he saw was one of our neighbors about my age and dressed similarly, with dark hair as I had. Although this was afterwards explained to him he would not allow me to remain, saying that I had already come into contact too much with the country children, and he would send me to boarding school. This is told to show his exclusiveness.

The younger children continued to attend Mrs. Bridgman's school, however. Mrs. Bridgman's husband is a brother of Laura Bridgman, the famous blind deaf mute known all over the world. I have seen several letters written by her to her brother in a square, peculiar hand used by the blind.

1861 (fall of Beaufort, South Carolina). Early in the fall of 1861 Port Royal Harbor, South Carolina, was threatened by the Union gunboats, and November 7th Forts Beauregard and Walker, situated respectively at Bay Point and Hilton Head, were captured. Their capture was followed by the evacuation of Beaufort the next day, and very soon that town was occupied by U.S. troops.

Brother Robert Oswald was then stationed at Ft. Beauregard, being a member of the Beaufort Volunteer Artillery, commanded by Captain (afterwards General) Stephen D. Elliott. When it was found impossible to hold the fort longer, Captain Elliott gave the command to retreat with tears in his eyes, so bitter was his disappointment and the humiliation. But the fort proved no adequate defense against the powerful guns of the U.S. warships. Our troops made their escape by [bagging] over the marsh to dry land under cover of darkness.

Brother Robert sent a hurried message to his wife (sister Anna) to leave the town immediately. This she did as well as every other woman, man and child in the town. Sister Anna got into her carriage and drove off with her baby (Henry) and such things as she could hurriedly gather up, leaving family bible, portraits, heirlooms, furniture, bedding, china, and even clothing, just as they were, some in her home in the town of Beaufort, and some in the plantation house a few miles out. She never saw them or her homes again. *Everything*—plantation, houses, stocks, crops, furniture, &c, &c—was captured or taken by the Yankees and negroes. The land was confiscated and has never been returned or paid for, & probably never will be.[35]

Such is the hard fate of war!

Some of the slaves lost at this time belonged to mama's "trust" estate. At this time sister Anna had five children, Robbie, Livie, Rosa, Dade, and Henry, but the oldest had been taken by her up to our house in Screven County upon mama's earnest request.[36]

---

[35] In her "Reminiscences of Trying Times," Georgia Lawton Morgan wrote that her sister Anna Oswald fled Beaufort with only with some clothes and silverware. After the war, when her husband Robert Oswald returned to his plantation Jericho (called "Jerico" by Cecilia), having walked home from a Northern prison, he found a dozen black families living there. "It had been in the Oswald family for several generations," Morgan wrote. "It was confiscated by the United States government, as also was his 'town house' in Beaufort" (in Miller, *Our Family Circle*, 360).

[36] The oldest Oswald child was Robert Lawton Oswald (1850–1918).

As soon as Beaufort was threatened, papa wrote urging brother Robert to move his family, his slaves, and all of his moveable effects (horses, mules, cattle, furniture, implements, &c, &c) up to Screven, offering him the use of the "Sharpe Place," an adjoining plantation owned by him which was comfortably settled. It had a sweet, pretty cottage house sitting in a grove of trees, & sister Anna could have been very comfortable there having papa within a mile to look after her and the plantation. But brother Robert said that no one else had moved off, and he decided to have them remain. A disastrous decision, as was afterwards proved. Had he done as papa wished, his family would have remained at a comfortable home, as good as their own, for it was their father's, all during the war. Moreover, they would have saved many of their effects at least until Sherman's army passed through Georgia, Screven County, in December 1864, when all was destroyed that came in their way.

Finding that sister Anna would not move herself or her belongings to Screven, mama then wrote her that if she would risk her own life by remaining in Beaufort she should not risk the children's, and that she would go after them if she did not send them at once to her.

(Dear old lady! How precious these grandchildren were to her!)

Upon this sister Anna brought them, leaving the 4 oldest and their nurse with us. Robbie and Livie, and later on Rosa and Dade, were entered at Mrs. Bridgman's school with Aleck and myself. Dauda (Georgia) attended also when her eyes permitted, and Walter Livingston (sister Rosa's son) whenever he was with us.

Livie was a very bright scholar and advanced rapidly, but Robbie was too full of fun and mischief to study much. Still, he was somewhat of a favorite with Mrs. Bridgman.

Brother George (Dr. George Baskerville Douglas), who had been stationed at Savannah, Georgia for several months at the outbreak of the Confederate War, was now in Virginia and had not been home since leaving Georgia. In April 1862 he came home on furlough to see his family, but met papa, sister Rosa and Georgia on the cars, they having just started for Charleston, S.C., to consult Dr. Geddings about Georgia's eyes.[37]

Brother George had shaved off the full beard he had worn, and with only a mustache, and in his full major's uniform, was not at first recognized. In fact he had kissed his wife and taken a seat beside her before she knew who he was. This was always a great joke on her, but she had seen papa looking on and smiling (for brother George had met him first) and supposed it was some near relative.

The whole party returned home where brother George was introduced to us as "Major Baskerville." This rank was that of surgeon major, & his middle name served as a disguise which however was soon penetrated.

It was always a joyful time with us when one of our soldiers came home on a short furlough, and they were made much of. Our house was the "home" of 4 soldiers. Brother George & Robert (Dr. Douglas & Mr. Oswald), George Douglas (son of Dr. Douglas by his first wife) and Dr. Bridgman, whose wife was our teacher.[38] Dr. Douglas was in Virginia during the greater part of the war, and Mr. Oswald & George Douglas were near the coast of South Carolina until the very last of the war, when they were sent to North Carolina.

When the war broke out George Douglas was going to school in Virginia (at Culpeper Court House, I think). He ran away from school and joined the Black Horse Regiment of Virginia.[39] He was only about 16 years old, perhaps 17, and his father

---

[37] Dr. Eli Geddings (1799–1878) was a prominent Charleston physician and a professor at the Medical College of South Carolina.

[38] George Craighead Douglas (b. 1844), the son of Dr. George Baskerville Douglas, served in Kirk's Rangers as a sergeant. His father's obituary stated, "He was captured late in the war and confined in a damp cell at Fortress Monroe, Va. He was never well afterwards. He married, however, and left one son, Lieut. R. Spencer Douglas" ("Dr. G. B. Douglas, Surgeon, C. S. A.," 83–84).

[39] This was a nickname for the 4th Virginia Volunteer Cavalry Regiment, organized in September 1861.

applied to the proper authorities and got him out of service, as he was under age. Later on he joined Kirk's Cavalry so as to be with Robert.

Poor Dauda (Georgia) had much trouble with her eyes from time to time, and her health was always poor. She was *much* indulged on account of this, and no rules of punctuality &c were forced upon her, while the balance of us (the children) were expected to be promptly at meals, at school, &c. Papa devoted his life to Dauda, reading to her when he was in the house, administering her medicines, treating her eyes, and devising every pleasure for her that she could enjoy harmlessly.

Noble, devoted father that he was! And yet alas! all this changed under the influence of a selfish, exacting woman (his second wife).

November 31st 1862 was Dauda's 17th birthday, and mama invited the Singelltons and Hobbys (the only near neighbors we were intimate with) to dine with us.[40] Poor Dauda sat in a darkened corner of the parlor with a large green silk shade over her eyes, and was suffering a great deal all day.

Mrs. Singellton ("Cousin Lizzie") & Mrs. Hobby told us of several wonderful cures of sore eyes made by Dr. Eli Geddings of Charleston & urged papa to take Dauda to him. The guests left about dusk, and I (a girl of 14) was racing about the yard as usual in the enjoyment of full and perfect health and spirits, when I had occasion to go up to my room, which I and Dauda shared together. The room was dark, but I heard a low sob coming from the bed. There lay poor Dauda weeping out her despair in solitude. I threw my arms around her and tried to comfort her.

"I am going blind!" she wailed. "I know I shall be totally blind. And it is so hard to submit, just as life is opening out before me!"

---

[40] The Hobbys were likely the family of Judge Wensley Hobby (1831–1892) of Sylvania. His wife was Gertrude Livingston Hobby (1826–1890), whose sister Ellen became the second wife of Cecilia's father Robert Themistocles Lawton.

I soothed and petted her and tried to inspire her with hope, telling her she must go to Dr. Geddings. But she had been to many physicians & some eye specialists who *tortured* her with severe operations, and got worse instead of better, and so she declared she would never let another doctor treat her eyes.

I went downstairs and told mama & papa of Dauda's distress and despair. The whole family used their influence in persuading her to try Dr. Eli Geddings, and finally she consented.

She had started off for Charleston with papa, sister Rosa, and her maid Delia, when they met Dr. Douglas. They returned home so as to see something of brother George, but a little later in the spring made the trip, brother George himself advising it. That wonderful old man, Dr. Eli Geddings, whom nature seemed to create for a healer of men's bodies, diagnosed her case correctly at once and applied the remedy. Instead of remaining in Charleston for weeks or months (as papa had expected), they were there only two or three days (at the Charleston Hotel, which was by far the best in the city). Dr. Geddings said Dauda (Georgia) could take his treatment just as well at home and would be better there. In the course of about two months her health and her eyes were quite restored. Wonderful we considered it, after so many others had failed. But Dauda never was as strong and robust as I was, I who never had an ache or a weakness of any kind, and longsuffering had made her nervous.

In August 1862 papa took Dauda and me to Indian Springs, Ga., Mrs. Bridgman going with us. Sister Anna's sixth child was born at our house August 7th and named for brother George, his full name being George Douglas Oswald.[41] The day after his birth we left for the springs. We enjoyed the trip very much.

Mama remained at home as usual to look after her large household and especially to care for sister Anna and the little baby. Papa often tried to induce her to travel with him, but she always

---

[41] The gravestone of George Douglas Oswald gives his birth date as August 7, 1862. He is buried in the graveyard of James Island Presbyterian Church.

said that she preferred to spend her share of the money in her home. As he always travelled in first class style, staying at the finest hotels &c, it seems to me that she should have received more than she did to spend on her home.

We had servants in plenty, pleasure horses in abundance, entertained a good deal (guests from a distance, as we visited *few* in the neighborhood), and kept a bountiful table of all that an old time plantation raised, and all that could be purchased, but the house was not fitted up in the style dear mama wished, as she loved to have beautiful things about her.

We raised our own rice, corn, vegetables, fruits of almost every description, cured our own hams (and they were delicious!) and bacon for the negroes, made delightful sausages, hog's head cheese, &c, raised our own turkeys and chickens (hundreds of them), killed our own home raised beef and mutton, made quantities of milk, cream, butter, &c. The products of the dairy and the eggs were often more than we could consume, but mama gave the surplus to her poor neighbors. It would never have occurred to her to sell them. Papa also made an abundance of syrup and sugar for the whole plantation, as well as our family.

During the war he planted very little cotton, for patriotic reasons, believing that the strength of the South lay in producing an abundance of foodstuffs. He planted enough cotton to clothe his negroes, for it was impossible to buy clothing & blankets &c for them during the war. Our ports were blockaded, & there were *very few* cotton factories in the South.

Mama learned the art of spinning and weaving and had several of her slave women taught. Six or eight of them (perhaps more) were kept busy all the time at their spinning wheels, & 4 looms were also kept going. One of the large rooms in our dwelling house was given up for the looms. Thus our slaves were clothed during the war.

At the outbreak of the war, "homespun" cloth made by hand was not a "lost art" in Screven County, nor in many other Southern communities, and this proved most fortunate at that time. The poor country women who understood spinning, dying and weaving found themselves in great demand both as teachers and producers. Mama hired one of them to teach her slave women these things, and to assist with the weaving.

"Marah," our black mammy, being the most intelligent of the slave women, was put in charge of the looms. Previously she had been mama's "right hand" in the housekeeping and in all fine sewing work, and mama made great sacrifice in giving her up for their work.

Lights were hard to provide during the war. Mama had tallow candles made in tin molds on homespun wicks which took the place of the oil and alcohol lamps previously used. But before the war closed we were glad to get even a long wick (which had been dipped in melted wax & tallow) wound around a bottle, to read by. One end rose a few inches above the mouth of the bottle to which it clung by adhesion, but every few minutes more had to be uncoiled as it burned rapidly, & would soon reach the bottle! Sometimes we were reduced to reading & sewing by firelight.

In December 1862, I & Dauda visited relatives in Lawtonville, South Carolina, spending Christmas (never then written xmas). While there I received my first proposal of marriage (D.P.). (I was 15 on December 11th.) I was so inexperienced & so unaccustomed to the companionship of strange boys that though I had good ideas of dignity in dealing with them, I was too nervous and sympathetic to refuse him decidedly as I should have done. I therefore left him half in doubt.

On my return home I made my sister Georgia (Dauda) a confidante, but afterwards regretted it when I accidentally overheard her telling papa of it. I was teased a great deal by them about this beau, whom they did not consider my equal.

During the whole of this year Richard Reynolds, an orphaned nephew of brother Robert Oswald's whose family had lost *all* (a large fortune) at the fall of Beaufort, was given a home &

schooling with us by papa.[42] During the winter of '62–63 sister Rosa bought a plantation near Halcyondale, #5 Central R.R. in Screven County & about 15 miles from our home. She moved there in January and had all of her slaves there also. She called the place "Bonheur."

1863. In January of this year both brother George (Dr. Douglas) and his son George were home on furlough. George was cleaning his father's pistol one morning when he accidentally shot himself through the foot, breaking several of the bones. He was laid up a long time and ever after had a stiff toe. Rebecca Mathewes was on a month's visit to us then, and used to help us nurse him.

During the spring I had my second offer of marriage (G.C.D.) and while on a visit to Lawtonville, South Carolina, in June, my third offer (R.K.), and began to consider myself quite a young lady, though with no intention of an early marriage.

Sister Anna spent a part of this year (the first half) in South Carolina so as to be near her husband, who was stationed at McPhersonville on Charleston & Savannah R.R. She boarded in Lawtonville until summer and then went for a while to McPhersonville, but the older children remained with us attending school.

Annie Douglas was born at "Bonheur" November 5th.

About the middle or last of March 1863, papa took Georgia and I to Albany, Ga. on a visit to uncle Joe and aunt Sally (Col. & Mrs. W. J. Lawton).[43] Uncle Joe was a colonel in the Confederate Army but was at home during our visit. They lived in handsome

---

[42] Richard Reynolds Jr. was the son of Richard Reynolds (d. 1861) and Ann Oswald (1825–1859), who was the sister of Robert Oswald, Cecilia's brother-in-law. In October 1863, at a very young age, Richard Jr. enlisted in the Beaufort Artillery, and just two days afterward, he was accidentally shot and killed by a fellow soldier at a camp near McPhersonville, South Carolina. The details of his death are described in *The Leverett Letters*, edited by Frances W. Taylor, et al.

[43] Winborn Joseph Lawton's second wife was Sarah (Sally) Lewis, whom he married in 1851.

style and had two beautiful little daughters about 5 & 8 years old (Minnie & Willie).

On our way out there we met cousin Aleck (Gen. A. R. Lawton of the Confederate Army).[44] He was off on a brief furlough, and was visiting a plantation he owned near Albany where his wife then was. They were both very polite and attentive to us, and as were uncle Joe and aunt Sally during our stay.

My darling mother died August 12th 1863 after a brief illness of 10 or 12 days. The disease was some kind of stomach inflammation brought on it was supposed by a sudden check of perspiration after being overheated. She was on her way from church when this occurred though it was a weekday. She was buried under a beautiful young oak tree in the Sylvania Cemetery, where her remains still rest. Blessed be her dear memory!

Mama's health had been perfect for four or five years previous to her death, and she led an active, useful, unselfish life.

Sister Anna and Aleck (my brother) were absent at that time and were sent for. Aleck arrived the day before her death, but sister Anna did not get home until the night after. I had no idea that mama was so seriously ill, being only 15 years old, and the youngest daughter, and having been a little unwell myself for a few days, I had no part in the nursing.

Early one morning I was called down to her deathbed. She was unconscious and passed away without speaking again. But it is a blessed remembrance to me that even the day before she had embraced and kissed me many times, calling me by the sweetest & most endearing terms. And I had repeated to her the 23rd Psalm beginning: "The Lord is my shepherd, I shall not want," little realizing that she was even then passing through the valley of the shadow of death. But we had the blessed assurance that she

---

[44] Cecilia's cousin Alexander Robert Lawton (1818–1896) lived in Savannah, Georgia, where he worked as a lawyer and was also involved in railroads. He was commissioned as a brigadier general in the Confederate Army in April 1861 and was later the quartermaster general. His wife was Sarah Gilbert Alexander Lawton (1826–1897).

"feared no evil," for her last whispered words caught by papa were "The master calleth, and I am going home."

Blessed, saintly Christian woman! Gentle, refined, Southern lady! Kindly friend, mistress and neighbor, devoted, *most devoted* wife and mother—all of these and much more she was, as all who knew her can testify.

Oh! that I might be like unto her, even in the smallest degree.

Even now, I cannot write of her death without the most poignant grief. (Her death seemed the beginning of disaster to our family, making as it did a stepmother possible.)

Dr. Douglas (brother George) happened to be at his plantation (on furlough) "Bonheur," and papa sent for him, so that we had the comfort of his attendance upon mama. Sister Rosa also came.

The house and yard was full of wailing negro slaves who had left their work in the fields and hastened from every part of the plantation upon hearing of the approaching calamity. As the breath left the beloved body, their sobs and wails suddenly became louder, for several of the older women had even entered her room, where we all stood around her bed. These humble friends and slaves bemoaned her loss and repeated over and over to each other her numerous kindnesses to them.

"We nubba git nudda (another) missus lik him (her)," all said.

They followed the body of their beloved mistress to the grave, and I remember that all whom we passed on the road thither (4 miles off), white or black folks stood respectfully beside the road with uncovered heads until the funeral procession had passed. (We had to send all the way to Savannah for the casket, brother George going for it.)

"Marah" (Mary), our black mammy, was mama's faithful & devoted nurse, and loved her and mourned her as her own mother.

Mrs. Bridgman, our governess, was also *more than* a friend to her. To this day she writes in *loving* & affectionate terms of our dear mother.

Indeed a wail must have gone up from some of our poor families around us when my darling mother passed away, for she had literally fed and clothed *many*, many of them. She made it her especial business to care for the wives and children of the poor soldiers. Often have I seen her start out with a one horse buggy loaded down with provisions, driving herself (though timid about horses), & with one of her children or grandchildren with her, or, if we were all in school, a small negro boy as "tiger" behind the buggy. Several times she got lost in the woods following a "blind path" to some poor little hut where she had heard there dwelt a sick or destitute family.

Will these not rise up in the judgment day & say, "Blessed art thou!"

Frequently several of the family went out with her in the carriage, but no amount of inconvenience, or even danger, deterred her from the work she had set herself to do.

Even now I recall just how she looked with tears streaming down her sweet sympathetic face as she listened to some tale of distress from these poor people, or as she came to us asking each one to share our purses and our wardrobes (made very scant by the war) with some destitute family. Both she and papa entered heart & soul into this work of providing for the soldiers' families.

During almost the entire time (since November '61) our family consisted of from 16 to 18 white people, and when "our soldiers" were home on furlough, their number was added to this. For this large family, and for frequent visitors from a distance who often paid long visits, dear mama kept house. She was the *ideal* head of a country home, always cheerful, industrious, looking after each inmate and each servant in person, caring for the comfort and well-being of all.

I look back in wonder as I recall all that she accomplished as hostess, wife, mother, grandmother, mistress, looking after sick negroes and infants, having negroes' clothing woven and many garments made up, providing for all the destitute neighbors *in person*, and above all, never under any circumstances neglecting her daily private devotions.

She spent a half hour (often more) in her private room every morning reading the bible and praying, and frequently this was repeated several times a day.

Mrs. Bridgman, who had been our private teacher, & living in our family for about two years, left us this summer and took a school in Sylvania. But our friendship continued as strong as ever, and during mama's illness she came to her bedside with words and deeds of love and devotion.

The two older boys required instruction in Latin and Greek, which Mrs. Bridgman could not give. Aleck (my brother) was sent to school in Allendale, Barnwell County, South Carolina, to Mr. Montague's school, boarding in his family. And Robbie Oswald (sister Anna's oldest) was put at a boy's school in Lawtonville, South Carolina.

October 1st 1863 papa took me to Augusta, Ga. and entered me at Misses Sedgewick's school.[45] They kept a large private school for girls but only 4 boarders, who made part of their family. I was one of these, & later on my sister Georgia completed the quartette.

I came home for Thanksgiving and also for Christmas, remaining about two weeks. Papa was taken desperately ill xmas day with pneumonia and I remained until the crisis was over. Dr. Douglas (brother George) was fortunately at home on furlough and so attended him.

The whole of sister Anna's, also sister Rosa's family, were with us during this holiday for brother Robert and George Douglas were also fortunate enough to obtain short furloughs. Sister Anna had not left our home since mama's death, and was keeping house for papa. Sister Rosa's home was now at "Bonheur" about 15 miles off, but she was often with us. During the early part of

---

[45] This was a school for young ladies operated by Maria Sedgwick (1828–1886) and her sister Betsey (Bessie) Swan Sedgwick (1823–1898), both of whom were natives of Connecticut. They later lived in Aiken, South Carolina.

this winter brother George was transferred from Virginia to Augusta, Georgia, so that I often saw him there.

During this xmas vacation I made the mistake of engaging myself to a very faithful and persistent lover (G.C.D.) who had known me since my 8th or 9th year. I knew him to be noble and honorable, and most devoted to me, and in an impulse of gratitude and self-reproach for my coldness, brought on by his deep feelings which he could not hide, I accepted him.

I had just passed my 16th birthday.

Then I set myself to the task of persuading myself that I returned his affection, and for a few weeks succeeded. Then came the discovery that I had made a mistake and could never love him save as a dear friend.

From this time I sought to get out of the engagement, and being [generous] and inexperienced did all I could to lessen his regard for me, hoping thus to rob the estrangement of its grief. I did not wish him to suffer through his love for me, and this was my method.

During my stay in Augusta I saw General John B. Morgan the great Confederate Cavalry leader & raider.[46] Dauda shook hands with him, but I was too bashful & held back. Immense crowds turned out to greet him. He & his wife boarded at the hotel "Southern States" just opposite Misses Sedgewick's.

In January 1864, Aleck (my brother) took me back to Misses Sedgewick's school in Augusta, papa being still too ill to leave his room. About a week or two later Dauda (Georgia) also came, being only a parlor-boarder studying French and Music and a few accomplishments. I began to have my voice trained by Miss Maria Sedgewick and took great delight in singing. It was one of the passions and yearnings of my life to sing well. But I was doomed to disappointment, for my marriage a few months later, and disastrous results of the war, robbed me of all such opportunities.

---

[46] This refers to John Hunt Morgan (1825–1864), a celebrated Confederate cavalry commander.

About the first of April Dauda and I returned home, and this was my last schooling. It was intended that I should "finish off" the next winter, but later events prevented this. Before returning home I had severed my engagement of marriage. Bettie Hammond (now the wife of Dr. W. R. Eve) the youngest daughter of George Hammond of Beech Island, S.C., was my most intimate friend while at Misses Sedgewick's.[47]

While in Augusta I had my fourth offer of marriage. (H.C.)

Colonel John McEnery of the 4th Louisiana Battalion (since governor of Louisiana) was our guest for several months during the spring and was joined by his wife, who remained until summer.[48] He had been desperately wounded and papa wanted him to come up while convalescing. Mr. & Mrs. Cy. Carter also paid a visit of several weeks in the spring.[49]

During this spring sister Anna engaged Miss Annie [Golding] as governess for her younger children. She was the daughter of that Presbyterian minister who wrote "The Young [Matroness]," a most charming book for children.

About the last of May or first of June sister Anna left for McPhersonville, S.C., to be near her husband, who was encamped at that place, and Dauda and I went soon after on a visit to her. Before we left, however, a sad blow had fallen upon us.

When we heard it (one Sabbath day) the whole household, children and grandchildren, were in tears, but, having regard for our father, we remained in our chambers and wept in silence. The governess (Miss Golding) discerned our general grief, and as I was

---

[47] This was Elizabeth Hammond (1849–1941), who was the daughter of James Henry Hammond (1807–1864). She married Dr. William Raiford Eve (1847–1916) in 1871.

[48] John McEnery (1833–1891) was a lieutenant colonel in the 4th Louisiana Infantry Battalion. His wife was Mary Elizabeth Thompson McEnery (1837–1904). He was discharged because of wounds in 1864. In 1872 he was the Democratic nominee for the governorship of Louisiana. Although McEnery took the oath of office in January 1873, the election was contested, and President Grant declared William P. Kellogg, a Republican, the winner.

[49] This may have been Cyrus Carter of Savannah, Georgia.

passing through the upper hall, intercepted me with a most anxious and sympathetic face, asking, "*Please* tell me, who is it that *is dead?*"

The absurdity of a marriage being mistaken for a death burst upon me with full force, and threw me into an hysterical condition in which I laughed and cried by turn.

Dear father, the most consistent, the most correct of men in all other respects, was about to contract a second marriage in less than a year after losing a wife whom he acknowledged to be a "pearl among women"—one whose wifely devotion had been the guiding star of [his] life for 32 years.

Moreover, his second wife (though devoted to him) was unsuited to him in taste and habits, being fond of frivolous amusements, vain, and sadly lacking in judgment. She was about 47 years old (a spinster), and papa was 57, a handsome, well-preserved man. That he fell victim to her well-laid plans, and caught him unawares, was proved by his own words to us immediately preceding the engagement, and by her actions in the matter.

Had he waited a reasonable time and chosen a wife better suited to him, his children would not have objected. As it was, we controlled our grief and tried to make the best of it. But she brought discord into a happy and united family. Papa had ever been a *most devoted*, *loving*, affectionate and *attentive* father, but she never rested until she had estranged him from his children and his grandchildren.

May God forgive her for the unhappiness she caused to him and to us!

About the first of June Dauda (Georgia) and I, with Dauda's maid Julia, went to visit sister Anna & brother Robert at McPhersonville, S.C., on Charleston and Savannah Railroad. We stopped over several days in Savannah with Mrs. Cy. Carter. Mr. [Humbol] Ogden and Mr. John Guerard were particularly pleasant to us upon this occasion.[50] We also enjoyed very much our visit to McPhersonville where we met a good many soldier boys from Beaufort and the surrounding coast. I remember best the attentions of William Drayton (son of General Drayton), young Hardee (nephew of General Hardee), Wilson [Neall].[51] We also saw a great deal of George Douglas, who was in the company with brother Robert—Kirk's Cavalry Battalion.

While we were in McPhersonville papa wrote us that June 28th had been selected as his wedding day. Sister Rosa had arranged to be at Blockade Place and receive the bride, and we decided not to go. But at the last moment, Dauda and I relented. It occurred to us that papa would be happier if we attended his wedding. So we hurriedly left with the maid, Julia, arriving at No. 6 Central Railroad after night. We tried to hire a conveyance to take us to our home 18 miles off, but could learn of none. After supper we retired to our room in the inn, which was kept by a very respectable gentleman with a wife whom rumor accused of being mentally deranged. It was not an inn, either, but they occasionally took in travellers as an accommodation.

The lady sent us about a dozen messages by a diminutive little negro girl warning us against the depredations of the rats, which she said swarmed through the house. Each message made us more and more nervous, and the final one—"Misses say you betta cubba (cover) you head, cause de rat'll run obah you!"—decided us to get up and remain awake.

Just about the time we had resumed our clothing a vehicle drove up and we were informed that two negro men had procured a wagon for us. On going out we were dumbfounded to find only

---

[50] John Guerard was likely Lt. Jacob John Guerard (1831–1864), a member of the 11th South Carolina Infantry Regiment, some companies of which were stationed at McPhersonville at various times. He was the son of Dr. Jacob Deveaux Guerard.

[51] The son of General Drayton (Thomas Fenwick Drayton) was William Seabrook Drayton (1844–1879), who served in Stuart's Company (the Beaufort Volunteer Artillery).

a rough plantation wagon "coupled" together, and without the pretense of a body. But the remembrance of the rat-haunted house decided us, and we set out seated on a rough board for sister Rosa's place "Bonheur" 4 miles off.

We arrived there after midnight & found that sister Rosa had left for Blockade Place, but we roused up her negro "driver" or foreman & had him get a wagon and two horses for us. This was the only vehicle left on the place at that time, and at least had a large body though without springs. In this plantation vehicle we reached our home soon after sunrise, taking papa completely by surprise. Sister Rosa and Aleck were already there, & uncle Stoney (Dr. James Stoney Lawton) arrived with his friend Mr. Montague later in the day.

The wedding took place that night, June 28th, at Judge Hobby's.[52] He was the brother-in-law of Miss Ellen Livingston (the bride). She was descended from Philip Livingston, signer of the Declaration of Independence, had been born in New York, and had many influential & wealthy relatives there, as well as in Charleston, S.C. Her mother was nee *Ashe* of Charleston, South Carolina.[53]

Dauda & I, with Julia the maid, returned to McPhersonville the day after (or 2 days?) the wedding. Aleck also came on a visit. It seemed the policy from the beginning for our step-mother to keep us away from home.

Before papa's wedding and while Dauda (Georgia) & I were at McPhersonville, it was arranged that we were to meet Bishop Elliott in Savannah, and Dauda & I were to be confirmed by him.

---

[52] This was Judge Wensley Hobby (1831–1892). A native of Augusta, he was an attorney and a judge in Sylvania, and for several years served in state troops and the Confederate Army during the war. His wife was Gertrude Livingston Hobby (1826–1890).

[53] Philip Livingston (1716–1778) of New York was a signer of the Declaration of Independence. His great-grandson, Philip P. Livingston (1791–1832), married Eliza Barnwell Ashe of Charleston.

Papa and sister Rosa went to Savannah to be with us, but the train left us, and thus Dauda & I were too late to meet the Bishop.[54]

I never had the opportunity again until after marriage when I was confirmed in St. Philip's Church, Charleston, South Carolina, by Bishop Davis, January 1868.[55]

Sometime between the middle and last of July we hurriedly left McPhersonville, for the Confederate troops there were ordered off to (where?), among them Kirk's Cavalry, to which brother Robert (Oswald) and George Douglas belonged. McPhersonville would thus be left unprotected, and could easily be raided by the Yankees, who were in possession of Beaufort and the surrounding country. Not knowing where to fly to, sister Anna went to Lawtonville about 20 or 25 miles distant, taking Dauda and me with her.

We all would have returned to our home in Screven County, Ga., which had been left to us by our mother, but papa and his new wife were living there, and we were given to understand that we were not wanted. It never occurred to us to insist upon our legal rights. In the meantime sister Rosa had moved to Columbus, Georgia, where Dr. Douglas, her husband, had been "post surgeon" in charge of all the large hospitals for some months past, in fact since early spring.

In Lawtonville, S.C., I met my future husband for the first time. He was a refugee, as were we. He had recently bought a large plantation near Lawtonville (6 miles off) and moved his slaves there, having been ordered to remove them from James Island by the Confederate Government in charge. He called upon us with one of our cousins, almost immediately after our arrival, and began paying me constant attentions at once, which however, I never imagined were serious.

It seems he was out of the army at that time, having recently recovered from a prolonged attack of typhoid malarial fever

---

[54] This was Episcopal Bishop Stephen Elliott (1806–1866).
[55] This was Bishop Thomas Frederick Davis (1804–1871).

contracted on James Island. At the outbreak of the war he had been in the Rutledge Mounted Riflemen.

I recall that his first visit impressed me rather unfavorably. He talked much nonsense, and I told my sister after he left that I could not decide if he was silly himself, or if he took me to be so. I afterwards found that he was intelligent enough, but fond at times of "talking wild."

He told me that he had a younger brother two or three years older than me, whom he would give me as a sweetheart, but before the younger brother arrived, he was pressing his own suit with me. He was himself 11 years my senior. He used to come courting in style, driving a very handsome pair of bays, with which characteristic humor he had named for two former sweethearts of his. His body servant Cain was always with him, dressed in a full suit of black broadcloth (for few affected liveries in those days).

About the first of September his attentions resulted in an engagement between us. It had been about six weeks since our first meeting. His proposal took me completely by surprise, and at first I supposed it was one of his many jokes. I had not seen him for about ten days, having excused myself several times when he had called. In part I had been furious with him on account of an attempted impertinence on his part. While driving with him, a pool of water caused him to turn out of the road. The buggy (or drag now called) jolted a little over the rough ground, and he jokingly passed his arm behind my waist saying he was afraid I would fall out. This I resented indignantly, and forthwith took a great dislike to him. His profuse apologies and explanations did not appease me, and I resolved never to receive him again. He had wounded my maiden pride greatly.

When we next met, it was by chance, and while I was visiting a cousin in the neighborhood. I treated him very coldly and was on my dignity, barely being civil enough to avoid attracting the notice of others.

The night was one of the most perfect I have ever seen, the moon making it as bright as day. We sat upon the high piazza of a noble country residence overlooking beautiful grounds. While he talked to me, his brother entertained my cousin. He remained so late that I was tired and sleepy, but he did not persuade me to give him the answer he wished.

Three days after, he came by appointment to receive my answer, which was a refusal. But this answer he would not take, and drew me into an argument which lasted from early afternoon until about one o'clock, and then he only left me upon receiving a halfway assent to his proposal.

Sister Anna, who was the pink of propriety, always remained up when Dauda or I had gentlemen visitors, and joined us from time to time. On this particular occasion both she and I tried ineffectually several times to induce him to leave earlier, but all of our polite stratagems failed. Of course sister Anna did not know the purport of our conversation, though she may have guessed it.

He now set himself to work in earnest to win my regards, and succeeded tolerably. Still, I was unwilling for him to speak to sister Anna on the subject, fearing that this would place matters on too serious a footing, and not yet being sure of my own heart. About the middle of September, papa and his new wife came on a visit to relatives in the neighborhood, and I objected for the same reason to his being approached on the subject. But in spite of my entreaties, Wallace would ask his consent to our engagement. After the interview, papa told me that he wished me to break off the engagement at least for a while. He gave me no reason, and as he did not like his authority questioned, I dared not ask him.

Sometime after my marriage he told me that Wallace was such a perfect stranger to him, and I so very young, that he desired it off for these reasons, and that he had told Wallace "he would let him know later on" what his wishes were. All of this was unknown to me at the time, but I did know that my stepmother had taken a violent and unreasoning dislike to Wallace, and was using her influence against him with papa.

After the above interview with Wallace, papa & his wife immediately returned to our home in Georgia, in fact on the very day. I was anxious to go with them, and so was Dauda, but our stepmother would not permit it. Thus we were cast off. We both (Dauda & I) wept bitterly when papa upheld his wife in this, and went off without us, and I have often since thought how different my life would probably have been had we returned home then. But I did as papa had requested, and wrote to Wallace breaking off the engagement.

He sent an answer, a note, by my messenger refusing to allow it broken, (I have always kept this) and followed his note in person in the course of an hour. I refused to see him when he called, but he remained and persisted until, through sister Anna's intercession, he succeeded in seeing me.

He was around again that evening, and by the *most persistent* and *continued* persuasion, finally got sister Anna (and me) to consent to our marriage the next week. We were married the following Tuesday, September 20th 1864, in the evening.

As for me, I have never been able to comprehend how I was persuaded into it. I expected to marry him at some time in the future, but not then, and certainly not without my father's consent. Yet I did both, and greatly offended my dear father, whom, however, I cannot exempt altogether from blame in the affair. Had he not so entirely cast his children off, had he allowed us to return home, I should never have married without his full consent. His unnatural conduct, his complete subservience to his wife's wishes, were the chief arguments used by Wallace with sister Anna & me. Moreover, the unsettled condition of the country (General Sherman had just captured Atlanta, Ga., & was threatening to overrun the whole country), sister Anna being a refugee, &c, &c, were all adroitly used as arguments in favor of a speedy marriage by this ardent lover. He won sister Anna (good, gentle soul!) over completely to his side, and between them, it was all arranged, and I could no longer hold out against him.

I was only 16 years & 9 months old, and he was nearing 28 years.

The house in which we were married was rented by sister Anna from a relative of ours. It was large, handsome and comfortable, with large grounds around it, 4 miles from Lawtonville. N.B.: General Sherman's army soon after burned it.

Sister Anna gave us a *very fine* supper in spite of the short notice, meats of every description, as well as sweets &c &c. I was married in a white India swiss dress of exquisite quality, made with very full skirt, "baby waist" (short sleeves & low neck), as was the style then, and with a deep lace "bertha" falling from the neck. It was a dress I had worn once or twice before.

Of course there was no time for preparing a *trousseau* which was a great grief to me at the time, but as the war times made clothing very scarce for all, such impromptu weddings were quite in vogue. And the knowledge of this made me better satisfied. Having hurried me into marriage, my husband wished me to accept a trousseau from him afterwards, but I was too independent for this, and would receive nothing from him in that line for months to come.

With self-pity I look back upon my utter unfitness to enter the marriage estate. With the best intentions and resolves, but with no experience whatever of life in its sternest moods, I stepped from an irresponsible girlhood which had been carefully guarded and hedged, into the most responsible position a woman can hold. Even now I weep to recall the girlish figure as it knelt beside her bed that night, the innocent, pure young heart that prayed God to make her a good and faithful wife to the man who had just led her to the altar.

Oh! The pity of it all! The pity of it all!

And yet God has answered her prayer, has given her strength through all to keep the vows registered that night. For this I must be thankful!

Up to this time my life had been all gladness & sunshine and innocent joy, holding only the one great sorrow of my mother's death. Folks used to say it made them happy to look at me, for I was the embodiment of all that was bright and happy and healthful. As to the family, I had grown to be the idol of all. Papa only still petted Dauda the most. It surely is not vain at this distant date to say that I was considered to have grown up very handsome. My cheeks were very rosy & round, like ripe peaches, my eyes bright and sparkling with fun, my hair long, very dark & abundant, my figure slight, but plump. I weighed 136 pounds when married.

My sister Georgia and brother Aleck were both at my wedding, so that the only absent one of us was sister Rosa. Papa did not come, being displeased, though I wrote him of the approaching wedding, so that in no sense was it a runaway match. Aleck was attending school at the time in Allendale, Barnwell County, about 12 or 15 miles off.

The second day after my marriage, sister Rosa arrived from Columbus, Georgia. She had come the greater part of the way by private conveyance, and had to make a detour in order to avoid the Yankees, who were marching under Sherman into the heart of Georgia. She had come for Dauda & me, intending to put me at a finishing school in Columbus. But fate decided that she arrived too late to take me. Wallace danced a jig when he heard she was driving up. He knew what her intended mission was. She remained about two days and took Dauda back with her to Columbus.

We stayed with sister Anna a week and then Wallace took me to his place a few miles off. It had a fine, rambling [tract], very large and comfortable old house on it, *many* and *superior* outbuildings, and beautiful shade trees, as well as a large and pretty flower garden. The place contained about 3,000 acres of land, much of which were highly improved & very fertile.

About three months later (in January 1865) every one of these buildings were burnt to the ground by Sherman, & most of the shade trees destroyed also.

Our honeymoon was scarcely over when Wallace had to leave me and join the Confederate Army, but as his command was protecting the surrounding country, he came home every now and then for a day or a night. As I could not be left alone, he persuaded sister Anna (whose husband was then in North Carolina with his command) to move over and live with me. Our house had *more* than room enough to accommodate them all, and we managed to be quite comfortable, sister Anna being a first-class housekeeper, and the plantation having everything upon it in the shape of provisions, meats, dairy products &c, that such an exceptionally productive place could raise.

But this did not last long. Christmas found us packing up to fly from the advancing Yankee army.

Early in December Sherman's army had passed through Screven County, Georgia, on his victorious march from Atlanta to Savannah, destroying all before him, and was now preparing to do likewise by the country on the South Carolina side of the Savannah River.

My extreme childishness at the time of my marriage showed itself in various ways. For instance, the day that Wallace took me to his home, Dauda went with us to spend the day and assist me in arranging the house &c. Wallace's younger brother was also there, and when dinner was announced, of course I was expected to take my seat at the head of the table opposite my husband. With this new position, all the fearful responsibilities of the life I had entered upon seemed to loom up before me suddenly. I was completely overcome, and somewhat hysterical. It was some minutes before I could be persuaded to take my place, for some unseen power seemed to be warning me against it, and whispering of all the cares that would come with the position. I suppose my husband was disgusted, but he tried to laugh it off.

He had been warned by sister Anna that I was a mere child in feelings and experience, knew nothing of housekeeping &c &c, but had answered that he would make allowances for all of this, and as to housekeeping, "I have very competent servants, and do not expect to make her a housekeeper!"

A week after entering my new home, I was therefore much surprised to have Mom Celie, his old nurse and housekeeper, hand me a basket of keys, saying her master had ordered her to do so.[56] I soon found that as much was expected of me as if I were a woman of thirty and of vast experience. The same duties that had devolved upon my mother, as mistress of the plantation, as well as of the house, now fell to my lot. But I was all incompetent to fulfill them. What did I know of sick negroes and infants? Or even of providing clothing for the slaves? Which involved at that time having them spun & woven on the place. The most painful part of my duties however was the expectation that I should *manage* & *control* these slaves with whom I came into contact. I was only a child, and a tenderhearted one, who had known my father's slave but as playmates & humble companions, and the agony of my new position will be remembered until I die.

During the three months that I remained on this plantation we fed hundreds of Confederate soldiers, especially in November & December. Most of them, I think, belonged to Wheeler's Cavalry and were Western men from Texas, Kentucky, Tennessee, and other border states. And nearly all were dressed in blue uniforms captured from U.S. soldiers.

One very large room, about 25 feet large & built off at an angle from the piazza, was given up to the soldiers. There they sat by a warm fire during the day and slept at night. As there was only one large bed in the room, many would have to sleep on their own blankets on the floor. All were given an abundance of food—pork, bread, hominy and rice—also molasses. Coffee or tea we did not have, as they were scarce commodities those days. Their horses were fed, their clothing washed (we kept several women busy at this), and (what seemed to delight them most), their knapsacks filled with ground nuts, which they called "goobers." Thus we learned the fondness of Western men for ground peas, of which Wallace had an abundant crop.[57]

---

[56] The usual spelling of "Mom" in the South Carolina Lowcountry was "Maum," a Gullah term by which older African American women were addressed.

[57] Goobers and ground peas were other names for peanuts.

As a rule Wheeler's men were considered terrors, but they behaved beautifully to us. One day they saved our gin house when it caught fire. Probably, had we refused to feed them, they would have helped themselves, but soldiers in those days were compelled to do this or starve.

About the first of January 1865 or perhaps a day or two before, Wallace took Livie Oswald and me over to Blockade Place, our home in Screven County, Ga. Livie had been my chum and confidante for many years past. Although 4 years younger, she was in many respects more congenial to me than Dauda was, though the latter was not quite 3 years older. Livie and I were both "Tomboys"—healthy children, full of animal spirits, while Dauda was delicate and prematurely old.

While on a scouting party, Wallace had visited papa at Blockade Place just before, & also just after, Sherman's passing. On the latter visit, papa told him to bring us over to him, as the Yankees would not likely pay a second visit to a country where nothing was left to pillage and destroy. But when we arrived, my stepmother flew into a rage & said she wished Sherman had burnt the dwelling also while destroying the other houses. She resented our finding a shelter there even at that time, though the house, plantation & servants were ours, being a part of our mother's estate. Papa owned several adjoining tracts of land & a good many slaves in his own right.

In crossing the Savannah River on our way to Screven County, the landing swarmed with Confederate soldiers. The only steamer on the river was chartered for them. The river was "[booming]" and its waters much too high to be crossed by the ferry "flat" as usual. But at length Wallace prevailed upon the officers in command to give us a passage over. We crossed with our horses, double buggy, servant and baggage, and arrived safely at Blockade Place.

Soon after, the owner of this steamer (Captain Dillon) loaded her down with cotton which he had bought cheap for Confederate money and had hidden in the river swamp, and slipped through the lines down the river to Savannah. There he surrendered himself and his boat to the Yankee general, who allowed him to retain possession of the cotton. This he sold for a sum sufficient to yield him a comfortable fortune. Cotton was then selling for about 75 [cents] per pound. I have often wondered if he continued to prosper after this treacherous act.

As our stepmother was very unjust in her demands (so much so that I will not here perpetuate them), Wallace soon engaged board in Sylvania, 4 miles off, at Judge Hobby's for me. This was January __ 1865.[58] He could not remain with me, as he was under army orders, but could get off occasionally to look after his affairs and to see me.

Having a good deal of Confederate money on hand, Wallace purchased the old Sylvania Hotel with a good-sized tract of land extending back from it (about 100 acres). This property was made over to me in place of a marriage settlement, which had been promised voluntarily by him, but it was sold about a year after the war by Wallace, and I never insisted on my rights.

December 1864. On our own plantation (property of my mother's estate), the "Blockade Place," the destruction was almost complete, but the dwelling house, the negro cabins, and some of the barns and outbuildings remained, probably because surrounded by the enemy's tents. The entire left wing of Sherman's Army under General *Jeff Davis* (name of our Confederate president), camped on our premises.[59] They burnt our gin houses, carriage house, store rooms &c, also papa's lumber and cotton and corn & wheat mills, run by a valuable water power one mile from our home. He was never able to rebuild these, and this valuable "Mill Place" became almost valueless.

From our place, the Yankees carried off nearly 30 head of horses & mules, several hundred head of cows, sheep, goats &

---

[58] The underscores here and elsewhere indicate a blank space in the text; perhaps Cecilia meant to fill them in at a later time.

[59] General Jefferson C. Davis (1828–1879), a native of Indiana, was the commander of the 14th Corps in the army of General William T. Sherman.

hogs, all our poultry, smoked bacon (an *immense quantity*), corn, potatoes, peas, &c, and, as they could not carry off the syrup & sugar, after the whole army had eaten their full for two days, they emptied the balance on the ground & mixed it with the sand—about 30 barrels of syrup & 15 of good brown sugar.

They ransacked every corner of the house & grounds, stole all my father's clothing, my stepmother's jewelry & valuables, many of which had been in her family (Livingston of New York) for over a hundred years. The wedding ring of my great grandparents Singellton was *exactly* one hundred years old. They found it in papa's desk, & though he begged for that & a small locket with Georgia's and my pictures, the rude soldiers pocketed them.

A loaded pistol was held to my dear old father's temple to make him tell of imaginary hoards of gold coin buried by him.

1865 (trip to Savannah). Here occurred one of the most unusual episodes in my life. While I was boarding at the Hobby's in Sylvania, and during Wallace's absence, two Savannah ladies who were then refugees and living temporarily in Augusta, stopped overnight at this house on their way to Savannah. They were Mrs. Hartridge, wife of Colonel Alfred Hartridge of Confederate States Army, sister-in-law of Congressman Julian Hartridge, and a Mrs. Mollenhauer, who was a very intelligent and shrewd old lady, and reported to be quite wealthy.[60]

General Sherman, after capturing Savannah, had issued an order allowing country people bringing provisions into the city to sell to pass unmolested. I doubt if enough was thus brought in to pay for the trouble of [watching] the vendors, as he, Sherman, had already devastated the surrounding country and swept it clean of

---

[60] Julia Smythe Wayne Hartridge (1838–1884) was the wife of Major Alfred Lamar Hartridge (1837–1913). A biographical sketch states that he ended his military career in the Confederate Army as a colonel of infantry, but his name is not listed in Bruce Allardice's biographical registry of full Confederate colonels. There is a Mrs. Regina Mollenhauer (1802–1887) buried in Charleston, South Carolina. She may have been the wife of H. W. Mollenhauer, a Charleston merchant.

provisions. But it was under this law that these two enterprising ladies resolved to attempt to enter the city, disguised as "country crackers."

While discussing how this could be arranged, I entered into their plans enthusiastically, and was invited to join them. Being childish and inexperienced, I eagerly accepted, having no idea of the difficulties ahead. Indeed, none of us had.

We started from Judge Hobby's house in Sylvania (about 60 miles from Savannah) early one morning. Judge Hobby insisted upon our driving to Whitesville in his carriage, though I had a "double buggy" (drag, now called) and handsome pair of horses of my own. Mrs. Hartridge, Mrs. Mollenhaur and I were therefore in his carriage, and he drove us himself. A cart followed behind us with a little bacon (from that saved by Wallace from Sherman's Army) and was driven by a slave of Judge Hobby's whom he recommended as particularly faithful!

He *ran away that night* to the Yankees, stealing the money that had been given him to buy corn & fodder for the mule, and leaving the poor mule (which belonged to Wallace). He was driven all day on an empty stomach (unknown to us at the time) and died that night in Savannah in great agony.

We spent the night in Whitesville, about ___ miles from Savannah, on the Central Rail Road, but the tracks of this road was torn up and utterly destroyed at that time.[61] We were here most hospitably and generously entertained by a charming lady, Mrs. White, who refused gently, but with considerable dignity, to be remunerated.

In the morning, we were startled to learn of the disappearance of the negro who had driven our cart, and feared that he would inform the guards of our assumed characters, and that thus

---

[61] Whitesville was a village in Effingham County located about thirty miles from Savannah. Some Savannah residents took refuge here during the war. By the time of the war, Whitesville had been renamed Guyton, but Cecilia makes no mention of this. The main body of General Sherman's army passed through Guyton in December 1864 and wrought much destruction there.

we should be refused admittance into Savannah. But after some consideration, we resolved to proceed and take the risks.

Judge Hobby returned to Sylvania in his carriage (called then a *barouche*), and we three ladies started out unprotected on our perilous voyage. We had ___ miles to traverse through a most desolated and ruined country, over which Sherman's brutal army had advanced in unchecked license only a few weeks before. I can recall but three inhabited houses in sight of the road, excepting a *few* negro cabins, for most of the negroes had sought freedom in Savannah.[62]

Scores upon scores of blackened chimneys stood like silent, accusing sentinels pointing heavenward and guarding the ashes of once happy homes, where the laughter of children & the cheerful household noises were forever hushed. Miles of fences had disappeared, showing only here & there, a heap of charred wood with other evidences of camp fires.

Not a *living animal*—horse, cow, sheep, goat, hog, or even chicken—was seen on the entire route, but *hundreds*, yea, thousands, were seen lying dead and rotting on the roadside and in adjacent fields, for it was Sherman's policy to have all such killed that could not be taken with his army to Savannah.

Vast droves of cattle of every kind, produced in this section, were driven into slaughter pens when they reached Savannah, & served to feed his army and the horde of negroes that accompanied them. All that escaped *en route*, or were accidentally left behind, were shot down.

As every farm and plantation furnished fresh horses, these animals were ridden until broken down, and then shot.[63]

---

[62] Cecilia and her companions were traveling southeast through Georgia from Sylvania (in Screven County) to Whitesville (or Guyton, in Effingham County) to Savannah (in Chatham County).

[63] Newspaperman John T. Trowbridge wrote of this practice, "Whenever fresh horses were taken, the used-up animals were shot. Such also was the fate of horses and mules found in the country, and not deemed worth taking" (*The South*, 478).

We found two "slaughter pens" of dead horses, where hundreds of decaying animals gave out noisome and putrefying odors extending for one or two miles in every direction! We could scarcely endure to breathe the air, and learned that the few inhabitants who were still living near these unfortunate localities had been obliged to fly from the pestilential odors. One of these pens was a country graveyard, and adjoining a neat little church! It seems too monstrous to believe, but I am writing only of what *I saw* myself.[64]

These inhuman Yankees had driven herd after herd of horses & mules into the graveyard, shooting them by scores, until they were piled one upon another, *entirely* filling the small enclosure and covering the sacred graves of their dead fellow men![65]

In several places we saw dead and putrefying bodies of men near the road. Most of them were negroes, camp followers, who had perished miserably from smallpox or other disease, even after gaining their newfound freedom. In one place the body of a white man, in blue U.S. uniform, lay close beside the road, almost in the wheel track, and everywhere the loathsome buzzard circled slowly above, or perched gloating upon his unresisting prey.

But the recollections, even now, sicken me. The country was one vast region of *silence, desolation,* and *death*!

Before reaching Savannah, we practiced the "cracker" brogue, and had endeavored also dress as became the characters we were assuming, that is, country people coming to town to trade the products of our farm for fine clothes, &c. But the U.S. major (German, without doubt) who met us at the outer line seemed

---

[64] This may have been the Little Ogeechee Baptist Church. One of Sherman's officers, George W. Nichols, stated that on December 6, 1864, the army had been concentrated at the "Ogeechee Church" for two days (*The Story of the Great March*, 81).

[65] These were large numbers of animals that had been captured or confiscated from Georgia citizens or Confederate troops, herded along together, and then shot to death all at once. In his retelling of this portion of Cecilia's memoir in *How Grand a Flame*, Clyde Bresee erroneously states that these horses "had been driven until they dropped" (110).

suspicious, and refused to pass us in. At last he consented for *one* of the party to pass, leaving the other two as hostages. Mrs. Hartridge then drove into town, leaving old Mrs. Mollenhauer and me at the outpost. It was Sunday afternoon, & some of her fashionable friends coming from church gazed in wonder at the handsome countrywoman seated on her cart, who looked so like their friend Colonel Hartridge's wife!

Mrs. Hartridge succeeded in getting a permit for us to enter also, and sent it to us by one of her friends. I was indeed thankful and relieved when the pass arrived, for my elderly chaperone had been drawn into a very heated argument with the negroes on guard on the subject of slavery and the negro race, and had made him furious. Besides, he showed a disposition to gaze too long and too impertinently upon me, and made some remark about my rosy cheeks, though I scarcely spoke to him.

Upon our return to Beaufort District, South Carolina, we found our fine old home gone. Sherman's Army had passed through that section in January, leaving ruin and desolation behind him. All left of our comfortable house was 7 stacks of chimneys and a heap of ashes. *Every* building on the place (16 in all) was destroyed by fire *save only* those negro cabins that were quite distant from the dwelling house. (There were 12 to 16 of these, well-built and comfortable for negroes.)

All of the barns, stables, carriage houses, gin houses (with engines, gins, &c) store rooms, "smoke houses," butcher house, servants' quarters for house servants, were of the most commodious and substantial build, and were therefore an immense loss.

Let none save those who have suffered likewise presume to judge of the grief and *just* indignation which swelled my heart about to bursting as I gazed at the ashes of our house, so wantonly destroyed by a vindictive foe.

The ruin wrought by that one man, Sherman, in the Southern states will not be repaired in a 100 years, and some such as destruction of records, books & heirlooms, can never be made good. Had he taken or destroyed only provisions, animals and cotton, no one would have blamed him, but the destruction of homes with their personal treasures, injured the whole country, and did not benefit his cause. But we were no worse off than our neighbors for there was scarcely a dwelling house left in the country.[66]

We had left sister Anna & her children (except Livie) in our house, but in his anxiety her husband procured a short furlough, came home, and moved them to Barnwell village, where his mother and stepfather (Rev. H. D. Duncan) lived, and there they were when Sherman's Army passed.

Wallace had been smart enough to save his horses, mules, cows, sheep, and meat. He had a quantity of pork meat, bacon, hams, lard &c, having just killed all his hogs. They were all driven over to Screven County until the Yankees had passed over our section of South Carolina going northward, then he brought them back to his plantation near Lawtonville, S.C. Of course he had left quantities of corn, rice, ground nuts, potatoes, &c, &c, also poultry and some cotton, all of which were burnt. But though we had provisions, we had no comfortable home to live in.

Wallace therefore procured board for us about 2 miles from our home at Mr. Stokes, an old countryman who lived in the "forks" of the creek, and thus had escaped a visit from Sherman's men.[67] He was a prosperous farmer, extremely well off, and lived comfortably. He had a large family among whom was a very pleasant and well educated daughter about my age. (She afterwards married Lawrence Youmans, her cousin.)[68]

Here I made up my new dresses bought in Savannah in which I took great pleasure, as *new clothes* were rarely seen in those dark days. Wallace was with me "off and on" as he frequently had to do scouting duty. Mr. Stokes' house was the *rendezvous* of all the

---

[66] Cecilia was referring to the area of Beaufort District, South Carolina, through which Sherman's army passed.

[67] This was Arthur Russell Stokes (1812–1895).

[68] Mary Ann Stokes (1847–1885), daughter of Arthur Russell Stokes, married her first cousin Laurens Winkler Youmans (1844–1908).

Confederate scouts in that section, as it was the *only place* within 30 to 40 miles where feed for man and beast could be obtained.

The harrowing tales told me by some of these scouts I shall recall with a shudder to my dying day. As a rule they were men who had been driven to desperation by the loss of kinsmen, homes, property, and were about to lose the cause for which all these had been sacrificed. They had practically "raised the black flag"—a measure which was then being generally discussed in the Confederate States. I believe that humane man, Robert E. Lee, opposed it.

As spring advanced, darker and darker grew the atmosphere, and fainter and fainter the flame of hope flickered in our devoted hearts. Our glorious cause was sinking to earth, dying amid the glare of ruined homes, the belching of cannon, the flaming of powder, the gore of its martyred heroes—and the mighty wail of a heartbroken people rose up as incense and consecrated it!

Even now the unbidden sobs will not [down], but rise up to choke and blind me as I recall the *saddest of all sad days!*

February 17th 1865 General Sherman captured and burned Columbia, S.C.

February 18th Charleston, S.C. was evacuated by our troops, and General Gilmore marched in and took peaceable by land.[69] It had been besieged by its water approaches for *4 years*, but had defiantly held its own. Now, however, that the whole of the surrounding country had been captured and destroyed, nothing could be gained by holding out, and our troops were needed elsewhere.

March 17th 1865 our Confederate Congress at Richmond adjourned "sine die" and Richmond, Va. was evacuated.[70]

April 8th 1865 the Yankees occupied Richmond, Va.[71]

April 9th General Robert E. Lee surrendered with his whole army. Surrounded, outnumbered by better fed, better clothed men

---

[69] The Confederate forces evacuated Charleston on February 17, 1865.

[70] The Confederate Congress in Richmond, Virginia, adjourned on March 18, 1865. The Confederate government evacuated Richmond on April 2, 1865.

[71] Union troops occupied Richmond on April 3, 1865.

than his, what else could he do? ___ thousand ragged and half-starved men surrendered to ___ thousand well-conditioned and better equipped men, after four years of the bravest fighting the world has ever seen.

And yet the civilized world looked on and applauded!

As railroad and telegraphic communication in our section had been entirely destroyed, news from the front reached us slowly. I recall distinctly the first announcement of our final defeat that I heard, and the indignation and incredulity with which I received it. But we hoped and believed that fighting would continue beyond the Mississippi.

April 14th Abraham Lincoln, president of U.S. assassinated by John Wilkes Booth, brother of the great actor Edwin Booth. Truth compels me to say that we, with one accord, rejoiced at the tidings. Our defeat was too recent, too bitter in all its degradation, for it to be otherwise. We felt that *one* of the victors was gone, & there was one less to gloat over our fallen condition.

As soon as the news of General Lee's surrender reached us, Wallace decided that it was best to move to our plantation about 2 miles from where we were boarding. All that he could count on for making a living was there—his cattle, horses, &c, &c—and he feared the negroes would become lawless and destroy them. He also decided to put in a large crop of cotton, and succeeded in procuring enough seed from ___ for most of the seed, as well as the cotton itself, had been burnt throughout the country overrun by the Yankees. Had he made & gathered this crop he would have done well, as cotton was up very high in the summer & fall.

Wallace had one of his negro cabins cleaned out & whitewashed, and here, with a *very few* articles of furniture which the negroes had snatched from our burning home, we began our modest housekeeping "after the war."

It was about the ___ of April when Wallace summoned all of the negro men to meet under the wide spreading branches of a large mulberry tree near the cabin we then occupied. He stood upon a [cart] and addressed them, told them that the war was over;

that the president of the United States had emancipated them; that while he regretted it, he should submit to it as best he could; that they were now as free as he was; that he had no power to punish or correct them in any way; that he wished to be upon friendly terms with them, and should endeavor to be so; and that such as wished to remain with him until the end of the year, and work for him, should draw a third share of the crop.

They received his speech in sullen silence, and a few with such dark glances that I (from my cabin door) trembled for my husband's safety. But they dispersed in silence to consider his proposition of working for him under contract. These negroes were all most anxious to return to their native home on the sea island (James Island), but saw the force of their master's reasoning—that it would be better to return in December with money in hand than at that time penniless. In a few days they had all signed the contract, and were working under it.

Some of the most narrow-minded of the slave owners in the country spoke (at a safe distance) of mobbing Wallace because he told his negroes of their freedom! How foolish! They really knew it before, & a few days later *all* knew it.

We were now in a most lawless country. The Confederate States were no more, and of course there was no civil law. Neither had the United States yet established military law in our section. Every man therefore held his life in his own hand, and in looking back, it seems a miracle that we passed safely through that dark period—two whites only on a plantation holding over a hundred negroes who had just begun to drink of the intoxicating cup of freedom, and no neighbors near enough to call upon.

Nothing points more strongly to the docility of the race than the *comparatively* few (for there were exceptions) who committed outrages upon their former owners at this period. Excitable they are, but docility and homage to mental & moral superiority excel in them. But do not suppose that docility was allied with honesty in them. The negro was no sooner free than he began to argue that all his master's possessions were the result of *his* labor, and therefore belonged to him. Not being courageous enough to take forcible possessions, he reverted to lies and strategy. Every few days a fine, fat cow would be lost to us. One was found with her neck broken, another badly gored, and had to be killed. In each case these were butchered and eaten by the negroes. At length their number hinted at the truth to Wallace, but I warned him not to use any harsh measures to suppress these robberies, or his life might answer for it.

I regret to say that Wallace frequently forgot himself and administered corporal punishment to them. It was both wrong and dangerous, but the old spirit of command remained.

One bright, sunny day a few weeks after we had moved back to our ruined plantation, I was twisting some homespun thread on a spinning wheel (which I took a patriotic pride in managing), and Wallace was sitting in the door of the cabin reading, when I saw a squad of U.S. negro troops with bayonets presented charging at double-quick right upon Wallace. The book he held hid them from them, and I found myself *voiceless* through sudden fear, so I could not warn him. The clanking of their arms as they halted suddenly at the step, made him start to his feet. But with wonderful control, he showed no terror, and *sternly* demanded their business.

They hesitated a moment. Then one of them stepped forward and said, "We come to tell you all the slaves are free! You got no right to work 'em anymore!"

"I have told them they are free, and they are working under a contract!" answered Wallace.

Another man now stepped up and demanded, "Have you taken the oath of allegiance to the United States?"

Wallace told them he had not, and the troops then insisted that he should go with them to their captain. We found later that they had acted without authority both in visiting our place and in arresting Wallace.

As I could not be left alone, Wallace told them he must get his horses and buggy, and went out to procure them, followed by several of the troops. As our stables &c had all been burned, the horses were in an open lot within calling distance. Before going out of the house, Wallace had strapped a small pistol around his waist. One of the troops demanded, "What you goin' to do wid dat pistol?"

"It is for my personal protection!" replied Wallace.

When he left the house they continued to grumble about the pistol.

"He got no business wid it!" "I don't truss 'im!" and such remarks.

One said, "He mus' give up dat pistol!"

At last I said, "Why do you mind about one man with a pistol, when there are fifty of you, & all armed to the teeth?"

This speech infuriated them. Their freedom was too recent for them to bear the comparison.

"Shut you d— sass!" "We is as brave as any white man!" "Don't you der say we isn't!" they exclaimed, as a dozen glittering rifles were pointed straight at me. "Take dat back!"

I shall thank a kind Creator to my dying day that my courage rose to the occasion. At that moment I was *my father's child!* All feelings of fear vanished, and indignation and scorn controlled me. I stood erect before these brutal black men with flashing eyes.

"You *are* inferior to white men! Though they may be enemies, white men would not try to bully a woman!" was the answer I hurled back to them. "But I am not afraid of you!"

One of them who looked superior to his companions now stepped up from the rear and said, "She is right, boys! It is not brave to bully a woman!" and the others fell back muttering.

I was thankful that my husband had not heard their language, and seen them threatening me, for I knew he was hotheaded, and indeed we knew that we were at the mercy of these troops, who could have murdered us with impunity. Several such murders by ex-slaves and negro troops had taken place in our section.[72]

As I stepped into the adjoining room to get my hat and gloves, two of the negro troops stole a handsome silver cup of Wallace's and a very old and valuable cut glass scent bottle having silver cover, and a red morocco case. This latter had belonged to my grandfather Singellton's father or grandfather. It was a gentleman's pocket scent bottle.

We reported these robberies to the captain (white) and pointed out the men who were guilty. The captain promised us to return these articles, but he never did. And yet the war was over!

But to return! During the time my husband was absent from the house, the negro troops continued to talk to me, but made no more threats. Still their purpose was to intimidate.

"You see dat man dere!" one exclaimed, pointing to a black soldier with a most *brutal* countenance, "Well, he kill his master an his master son, and den run way an come to us! He cut open both dem with axe. His master been sleepin in his bed, and his son been sitting in front de fire!"

The murderer was *swelling with pride* as his deeds were recounted!

Another black brute in blue uniform was pointed out, who had come softly up behind his master in the field and split his head open with a hoe, and one or two others who were almost equally famous.

---

[72] On November 24, 1864, Beaufort's Union newspaper *The New South* published an account of the execution of two Federal soldiers, Private James Grippen (or Gripon), and Private Benjamin Redding, of the 104th United States Colored Troops who, along with other black soldiers, committed crimes in McPhersonville. They plundered two houses, raped several women who lived there, attempted to murder a male family member, and then burned one of the dwellings. They were court-martialed, found guilty, and executed on Hilton Head Island, South Carolina. Records of the crimes and executions of Grippen and Redding can be found in the "List of U.S. Soldiers Executed by the United States Military Authorities During the War" at the National Archives. The spelling of their names varies slightly.

These facts will give some idea of the [personnel] of the negro companies of the U.S. Army of that period.

Some of them, seeking to [tantalize] me said, "We are going to take all your colored people off. Now, *you looks mighty tinder, you* can't work! What you gwine ter do?"

I replied with dignity, "I am *very* strong, and can do any kind of hard work."

Poor child! My powers were tested and found wanting before many hours had elapsed.

It was curious to note the difference in the *language* of the negro troops. Some were upcountry negroes, and some lowcountry. Some had already gained a little education, and were trying very hard to show it in their speech. It seemed to me they were the *blackest* as well as the most brutal collection of negroes I had ever seen. Not a light-colored man was among them.

When Wallace drove up to the door, I locked up our cabin and got into the buggy with him. One of the black soldiers, in high good humor, jumped up *behind* the buggy just as our negro slave footmen (or "tigers") used to do! Yet Wallace was the prisoner and he the captor!

In this style we drove about two miles, when we came up with the white captain of our invading negro company, who released Wallace upon a verbal promise to take the oath of allegiance at his earliest convenience. This command was stationed at Robertville about 15 or 20 miles from us.[73] They were the nearest U.S. troops at that time and had visited our neighborhood to arrest a white farmer on the adjoining place for flogging an old negro woman. Well, he deserved it! But Wallace had, within an hour of their coming, struck and beat a young negro man for impertinence! The

---

[73] Although U.S. troops may have been stationed in that area, there was nothing left of Robertville after Sherman's army passed through it. In "The Life and Death of Robertville," Thomas O. Lawton wrote, "When the troops departed, a townsman wrote that only a fence pole remained to indicate where the village had once stood" (8).

troops knew nothing of this, and had no right to invade our premises. But *might* made *right* in those days!

Unfortunately for us, our negroes were all working near the
house that day. The crops of corn and cotton promised well, and
all were in tolerably good spirits. But the negro troops, in their
fine blue uniforms, ran to them calling out, "What you workin
for?"

"Ain't you know you is free?"

"Uncle Sam got nuff meat, en coffee, en sugar to feed you all!
An he got gold for you to walk on from yah to Beaufort!"

"You is fool to work any more!"

"Come wid us!"

The poor, deluded souls dropped their hoes and their plow
handles instantly, and in great excitement gathered up their children and fled on foot and empty-handed to the promised bounty.
In less than an hour's time, probably in 30 minutes, the plantation
was deserted! Not one remained.

"Meat, and coffee, and sugar," and *idleness*; how could they
resist these luxuries? Dearer to the negro's heart they are than all
others. As we passed them on the road as we were driving to the
captain, many of them bid us kindly adieux, and a few were in
tears, particularly old daddy Johnson, who was wringing his hands
and weeping. But his young wife was going and had taken his two
children, and he must follow.

When we next saw them the following spring upon James
Island, nearly all were pitted with smallpox marks, and had lost
many members of their families. They called this "de union mark"
(i.e. U.S.).[74] They left *comfortable* homes, good furniture, bedding,
utensils &c, corn in each house left to last for the balance of the
year, and a share in the coming crops—and went to face starvation, hardship and pestilence!

---

[74] In his recent study of African American suffering and illness during and
after the war, *Sick from Freedom*, Jim Downs makes the case that the federal government neglected the health of the freedmen in the South and did not respond
very effectively to the epidemics of smallpox and other sicknesses among them.

When Wallace and I returned to our home, a poor little two-roomed negro cabin, with a few articles of furniture, sundown was approaching. As we were the only human beings on that large plantation, we set about looking after our horses. The corn was in the shuck, which had to be removed, and as I was lonely and timid, I followed Wallace to the barn and helped him to "shuck the corn" which was in one of the negro cabins, for *every* other building on the place, & even some of these, had been burnt by Sherman's army.

As night settled down over the earth, terror took possession of my soul. I was no longer the heroic young woman, but a veritable coward. Accustomed always to the cheerful sounds of a large plantation—the singing and laughter of many negroes, the voices of children, crowing of cocks, &c &c. The *silence* of the place that night hung over me like a pall, and weighed on my soul. I recalled the blood-curdling stories told me a few hours before by those brutal-looking black men, and the fact that Wallace had that day beat Peter Brown, one of his former slaves. I knew that he could return with others who had real or imaginary wrongs to resent, and murder Wallace and me, and that no punishment would follow.

Besides, we had a little silver and gold money (about $135.00) *which was probably the only coin within miles of us* in that section, and also some silver plate saved from the Yankee raiders. The negroes knew of these, and robbery would be an additional incentive. Should I live to be one hundred years old, I can never forget the *terror unspeakable* of that night!

Wallace retired to his bed and insisted upon my doing so. But I lay down only a few moments. My hair seemed to stand on end, my soul quaked within me, and sleep was impossible. I rose and dressed, and implored Wallace to go to one of the neighbors. He at last consented. We took the coin. Wallace armed himself with his pistol and an axe, and we made our way through the woods about a mile to our nearest neighbors—a family of well-to-do farmers named Ayers. On the way, we started at every sound—the hooting of owls, the scampering of rabbits, &c. We passed near to a campfire which seemed recently built, but no one was in sight.

We routed up the Ayers, who had long retired, told them of the raid on our plantation, and of my terror. They kindly and willingly took us in for the night. Early the next morning, we returned to our plantation, refusing to remain to breakfast, which we were urged to do. We expected to find our cabin in ashes, and all our horses gone. But the place had not been molested. After that night, my terror *somewhat* subsided, but I have always dreaded a *desolated plantation.*

I attempted to cook some breakfast (another negro cabin next to the one we inhabited served as a kitchen), but I failed utterly. Neither Wallace nor I could eat the food I prepared. It was only hominy & fried bacon! There was no stove, only an open fire, and I burnt my hands and face over it.

Wallace tried to milk the cows (they had come themselves during the night). He came in disgusted with only a *small cup* of milk! Instead of two large buckets full. We sat down and laughed at each other, and Wallace declared that I should *never, never* cook another meal! (I don't blame him!) This was my first and last attempt at cooking, but Wallace afterwards learned to milk cows quite expertly.

We had eaten all the cold bread for supper, so we made our breakfast on peaches and some sour clabber. Kind Mrs. Ayer came over unbidden and cooked a beautiful dinner for us—vegetables, meat & bread—which served for three meals. She continued doing this for three days, at the end of which time Wallace had procured a cook by riding the country over. He also succeeded in hiring a *few* men to work his crops, but by far the larger area had to be abandoned, though up and growing well. He saved only a few acres.

Wallace had saved a large drove of sheep from the Yankees by driving them (across river?) until Sherman's army had passed. They were now very valuable, as all farm animals were scarce. But they disappeared just at the time his negroes did—doubtless driven off by some of the gangs of desperados who preyed upon the country in these lawless times, committing atrocities of all kinds.

Our soldiers were now slowly returning from the various places of capitulation. Those who had been scouting through our section (as Wallace and his brother Powell had) were among the first, of course.[75] Then those from North Carolina and Virginia, and more distant points.

Some who were in Yankee prisons were not released for several months. This was the case with George C. Douglas (brother George's son). The poor young fellow (only 20 years old then) had been starved, deprived of water and change of clothing, and closely confined in a damp underground cell at Fortress Monroe (Va.), and came home a physical wreck. He never recovered his health and died early in life.

Dr. George B. Douglas and Mr. Robert Oswald, my two brothers-in-law, returned to their families soon after the surrender—the former were fled to Albany, Ga., and the latter to Barnwell Courthouse, S.C., where her husband's mother & stepfather lived, the Duncans.

At this period there were no mails throughout our desolated section, and letters could only be procured by private means.

Our soldiers returned home, as a rule, ragged and half-starved. Many of them had even been robbed at capture of all garments save a [pair] trousers & perhaps a tattered shirt, and some were compelled to part with their garments for food as they journeyed through the sections raided by Sherman.

Footsore and weary they dragged themselves towards their homes—only to find them in ashes—ruined plantations, scattered families, the season far advanced for planting, but no crops, *no seed* corn even, no laborers, no food! And it was a rare exception when a horse or a mule could be procured to work a crop. Yet the most of these noble men rose to the occasion as best they could. Hands

---

[75] Winborn's younger brother, Josiah Powell Lawton (1846–1910).

71

all unaccustomed to labor seized the hoe or the plow handles, for wives and children must be fed. Late as it was, patches of corn, potatoes, peas—sometimes even a little cotton—were planted and worked with blistering hands. And our bountiful soil yielded kindly and saved our land from greater and widespread starvation.

But these were not all of the horrors our ruined country suffered. Many of our soldiers returned home in a desperate frame of mind, and really thirsting for blood! I heard two formerly good and worthy men say that the thirst for blood was almost uncontrollable in them. They had seen so much bloodshed for four years past, had suffered so much, and had come home to ruined homes to see their families suffer more. Their country was gone, and they were almost ready to believe that God had deserted them!

Besides, the *morals* of the men were corrupted. As soldiers marching through the country, they had often been compelled to capture their food or starve. The habit grew upon them. If a pig darted across their path, a pistol would be leveled upon it before the owner realized what he was doing. It was the animal, man, brought down to first principles, and the instinct to procure food asserted itself. I believe it was fully a year before these impulses were entirely checked, even in the most honorable returned soldier.[76]

Our lives were hard all during this year. Food was scarce and of the coarsest kind. We considered ourselves most fortunate to have some wheat flour and a little lard, corn meal and grit ground on a hand mill (all others had been burnt by the Yankees), and *above all else* some bacon! We also had a few vegetables and fruits, and milk & butter. As there were few cows left in the country, it will be seen how much better off we were than our neighbors. Fresh meat, or chickens or eggs we never saw!

We also had some money, for my thrifty husband had invested several thousand dollars of Confederate money *in tobacco*

---

[76] A note is penciled here: "Wallace urged to be a member of Ratification (?) convention."

just a few weeks before Lee's surrender. Now the average Southern farmer (not the large planters) will have his "chawin terbaccah" if his family is starving, and thus all the hoarded coins for miles around found their ways into Wallace's pockets.

Later in the summer, Wallace started a small store, utilizing another negro cabin for this, and made one perilous trip to Savannah by wagon to procure goods, accompanied by two others for protection. I had not seen *cheese* for four years, and *overate* my capacity on his return. For several years after I disliked cheese.

This store would probably have proved quite remunerative had it been continued, but unforeseen circumstances broke it up early in the autumn. It was the first store started in that section.

During the summer a company of U.S. soldiers (all white) were sent to Lawtonville and encamped there in the Baptist church yard under a beautiful grove of sycamores.[77] This was six miles from us. We were all most thankful when they arrived, for even military rule was better than no rule at all. All small cases of lawlessness were submitted to the arbitration of this captain. More serious ones were carried to the headquarters of that department at Port Royal.

I went on a short visit to Blockade Place, our old home in Screven County, Ga., with Wallace in midsummer. Sister Anna's family were there with papa, but kept her own table. Papa's negroes had most of them deserted the crops after they were planted (as Wallace's had). The poor old gentleman attempted to plow himself, but broke down at it. My only brother, Aleck, then only in his 15th year, ran out into the field when he heard of papa's attempt, and with tears in his eyes, begged papa to let him plow instead. But papa said he was physically stronger than Aleck, who was then small for his age. He afterwards grew to be a large and very strong man, being six feet tall and fine looking. Though the

---

[77] The village of Lawtonville was destroyed by Sherman's army in January 1865. The only building left standing was a church, which suffered some damages and was used as a hospital.

exact size of papa, he was not near so handsome! But few men were!

During this fall, there was much talk of a war between England and the United States on account of the "Alabama" claims, but England made concessions.[78] Had she only known it, the ex-Confederate soldiers would have gladly aided her to whip the U.S. But our lips were sealed by tyrant rulers, and even our newspapers would not have dared to advocate such a movement.

I pass over the fall months of this year as being too painful to recall.[79] Few girls of 17 have been called to endure all that I suffered. In looking back, the *one* consolation left me is that I acted throughout the entire ordeal in a perfectly *natural* manner, and that every impulse of my young heart was then *pure* and *right*. Therefore, I have never suffered since from the pangs of an accusing conscience in connecting with that sorrowful time.

I thank God, my kind guide & protector for this much!

During a short visit to Savannah in November, I purchased new clothing for myself and the coming baby, & considered myself fortunate to have such fine things. Money was so scarce that most of our people still wore the faded garments that had survived the war.

---

[78] The "Alabama claims" were a series of claims made by the United States against Great Britain for damages done to U.S. shipping by Confederate commerce raiders. The most famous of these ships was the ship CSS *Alabama*, which was fitted out in a British port and allowed to operate in violation of existing international law. The dispute went on for years but was finally settled in 1872 when a tribunal in Geneva, Switzerland, awarded the United States a large sum of money in gold.

[79] One very painful event took place in September 1865, when Cecilia's husband, Wallace, shot and killed his brother-in-law Asa Waring Lawton during a dispute over a property transaction. Wallace was arrested and tried in proceedings conducted by the occupying U.S. military forces on Hilton Head Island. He was found guilty of "excusable homicide" because he had killed Asa without "malice aforethought" (premeditation) and was therefore acquitted of the charge of murder. Details of the dispute, the shooting, and the trial are found in Bresee's *How Grand a Flame* (127–44).

In December, Wallace and I were at Blockade Place, Screven County, with my kind and loving sister Anna, and her equally kind husband (brother Robert Oswald). But we left about the first of the month for our plantation in Beaufort District, South Carolina, where Wallace gathered up the yield of his small crops, sold his horses, mules, cows, wagons &c, shipped his cotton to Savannah, and went himself down to Charleston to look after his property on James Island.

Steamboats began again running on the Savannah River about this time, and the Central R.R. of Georgia was patched up and running some *very dilapidated* cars. *Nearly all* their cars had been burnt by Sherman, and their entire track taken up, the iron rails *twisted* (by means of their cannon wheels) and the crossties burnt. The Charleston & Savannah, and the South Carolina railroads were likewise destroyed.

Wallace left me with sister Anna. She owned a plantation (Sylvan Home) about two miles from ours near Lawtonville, and they moved to this in December. They were about as destitute of furniture as we were, but their comfortable dwelling had not been burnt. It had been rented out during the war. Here my first baby, "Bertie," was born January 23rd 1866, and I came near losing my life by the most *brutal mismanagement*.[80] I had only an ignorant negro midwife to attend me. The nearest doctor charged $25.00, and to save this sum, my health was wrecked! Up to this time, I had enjoyed *perfect health* all my life. Dear sister Anna was as kind and attentive to me as she could be. Wallace was with me when the baby arrived, but soon returned to Charleston.

When my baby was just five weeks old, I went to Charleston and joined my husband. Powell Lawton and Robbie Oswald drove me with my nurse and baby to Blackville, South Carolina Railroad, where I took the train. The nurse "Mom Bess," a splendid servant, returned with them, but Wallace had a nurse engaged when I reached Charleston.

---

[80] Bertie was Robert Themistocles Lawton. He died in July 1867.

On the train were many ex-Confederate soldiers telling anecdotes of the war or of antebellum times. One Yankee only was on the train. He was *readily* designated by his brand new clothing, valise, &c, as well as by his harsh New England features and voice, though he scarcely spoke.

Finally the chief jovial speaker observed that he hated the Yankees so that he wished them not to come South on any terms, either as capitalists or as laborers. That he hated to be near them, and would avoid going to Heaven if he thought he would be doomed to meet them there! At this, the smart-looking Yankee gathered up his belongings and removed his seat to the farther end of the car, leaving the warmth from the stove in possession of the Southerners. The jovial ex-Confederate looked around the group with a benign smile and said, "I thought that would move him! *Now* we can enjoy our talk unmolested!"

This shows the feeling at that time.

Wallace had experienced much difficulty in regaining possession of his James Island property, & finally had to pay out several hundred dollars (a *big* sum then) to buy off the negroes who had "land claims" from the U.S. general & were on his land. Each had a claim for 40 acres, & the total made more land than Wallace owned! The general told Wallace he had *given the land to more loyal citizens*!

This was my first visit to Charleston, and I knew not one soul in the city save my husband. I was in poor health for the first time in my life, and I had a young infant to care for, so that the two weeks of my stay there were not pleasant. We boarded on Limehouse Street near the water.

One lovely spring day in the middle of March, Wallace took me over to James Island to live. Under happier conditions, I would have enjoyed the row across the river, but, as it was, I wept bitterly and silently the whole way and heeded none of the beauties of nature. With my babe pressed to my bosom, & a veil over my face, I approached my new home! Unhappy omen!

Wallace's large and handsome mansion on "Bennett's" plantation just opposite South Battery had been swept away by the war, with all outbuildings, trees, &c. Our own soldiers—those belonging to the "country cracker" class, who hated all wealthy planters, had wrought the destruction. Some of the places on James Island were destroyed by the Yankees also, so that from friends and enemies, that doomed island suffered the worst.[81]

Almost the only building left on his three James Island places was a small two-roomed cottage at the "Bluff." It was neatly lined with boards, had a porch in front, and was *tolerably* comfortable for those hard times. Here we made our home. In sight of the Bluff was "Cuthbert's" House, on one of Wallace's places, but it was badly out of repair, & *500 negroes had died in it of smallpox* during the summer & fall of '65, therefore we shunned it![82]

My poor little babe was ill when we reached James Island, and immediately became much worse. I had no experience, and did not know what to do. In my ignorance of medicine, I gave him a teaspoonful of laudanum! He went to sleep immediately and came very near to death. We sent for the doctor as soon as I told

---

[81] In a memoir written in 1888, Robert Elliott Mellichamp stated that Confederate soldiers destroyed a number of houses on James Island in "sheer wantonness." However, some houses and buildings on the sea islands near Charleston were eliminated by the Confederates for reasons of military necessity. According to Mellichamp, twenty-five houses near Fort Johnson were demolished by Confederate forces because they were located in the way of their fortifications. The little village of Legareville, located on Johns Island (just across the Stono River from James Island) was burned by order of Major John Jenkins in August 1864. An enemy battery and gunboat were shelling the village, and the Confederate forces burned it so that it would not be "useful to the enemy." The Episcopal church on James Island (St. James) accidentally burned in 1864. All the church's records had been sent to Winnsboro, South Carolina, but were burned there by Sherman's troops in 1865 (Mellichamp, "Sketch of James Island, South Carolina," 5).

[82] Dr. Joseph I. Waring noted that in 1865 there was a fearful smallpox epidemic on James Island, which had "almost entirely a Negro population, including many hopeful but starving refugees from other areas." There were 1,900 deaths out of a population of 4,000 (*A History of Medicine in South Carolina*, 40).

Wallace of the baby's long sleep, but he did not arrive until the next morning. He, Dr. Robert Lebby, said the child's life was saved by a miracle, as he could not understand it.[83]

Wallace, with his usual thrift, soon started a small store at the "Bluff" and sent for Robbie Oswald to clerk for him. He also made a little money nearly every day by taking passengers to & from the city in a *long* canoe boat called "Stark Naked" because of its trim appearance. He had recovered this boat from some negroes who had stolen it from his James Island place during his "refugeeing" absence.

All means were resorted to at this time to make an honest living. General Stephen D. Elliott, ex-Confederate, & once a wealthy planter, was then supporting his family at Beaufort by fishing! And we honored him for it!

The negroes objected to working for former slave owners at this period, so Wallace could plant no crops, but rented *part of his place* to a German for $1,000.00. This was thought a large sum, but cotton then sold high—$1.00 per pound for Sea Islands!

We had bought some new furniture in Charleston and made our little cottage tolerably comfortable, but my life was hard! In poor health, with a young infant who was often sick, with a husband whose health began to fail also, with the most incompetent and unreliable servants, with no conveniences for housekeeping, and no knowledge of the art, I was indeed an object to be pitied. My nights seemed to be spent in nursing Wallace (who was afflicted with boils) or the baby, and much of my days in weeping bitterly. Let no one accuse me of weakness—for none knows all the discouragements and sufferings I underwent.

I never a saw a white woman's face from month to month, for very few had returned from their refugee homes at that time. I heard that some ladies had returned to Secessionville, 6 miles off,

---

[83] This was either Dr. Robert Lebby (1805–1887) or his son Dr. Robert Lebby, Jr. (1831–1907).

but they had no means of visiting me.[84] No one could then afford pleasure horses or vehicles.

William Hinson & Elias Rivers, who were planting on the island, were almost the only visitors we had.[85] Sometimes the Yankee surgeon (Brownlee), who still remained to attend sick negroes, called.[86] He seemed friendly, & we treated him politely.

After over three months of this life, we moved to Charleston about the last of June, where we boarded on Legare Street at the Dill's.[87] Dr. Lebby told Wallace that he *must* take me away from James Island or the life would *kill me*!

It was like going from Hades into Heaven! Dear Mrs. Dill took the poor child wife and mother into her heart—nursed her, soothed her, cared for her baby, advised her—did almost all a mother could have done for her. Oh, the blessed comfort and rest I found in that spot, her well-ordered home!

Miss Hayes Rivers, an older maiden sister of Mrs. Dill's, was also devoted to me and my baby, but she was not so strong a

---

[84] According to Robert E. Mellichamp's historical sketch of James Island, Secessionville was a summer resort on James Island established by "five or six" island planters. The site was originally called Stent's Point, but renamed Secessionville, the "political agitations of the day (1851) suggesting the name" ("Sketch of James Island," 2).

[85] William Godber Hinson (1828–1919), a planter and agriculturalist, owned Stiles Point Plantation on James Island. Elias Lynch Rivers (1838–1911) planted at Centerville Plantation on James Island.

[86] This was Dr. Charles Henry Brownley. He was licensed to practice medicine upon graduation from the Queen's College of Medicine (Kingston, Canada) in 1862 and signed a contract to work as a physician for the Freedmen's Bureau in Washington, DC, in August 1865. Some sources say that he was later a postmaster in Colleton County, South Carolina. He was born in 1842 and may have been a native of England or Canada. In 1882, he married Annie Margaret Mikell, who was born in 1863.

[87] This was Joseph Taylor Dill (1822–1900) and his wife, Eleanor Caroline Rivers Dill (1825–1878). He owned Stono Plantation on James Island. Mrs. Dill was the daughter of John Rivers (1786–1856) and his second wife Eleanor Rivers (d. 1836).

character, or as intellectual as Mrs. Dill.[88] It is to the latter that I owe *much* in the way of good & sensible advice and training. Wallace respected her highly, and her influence over him (her father's Godson) was always a good & noble one.

The Dills took no other boarders, but having invited me to dine & attend church with them, took a fancy to me, and probably pitied my forlorn position! Little Gena, their only child, was devoted to me also.[89]

We had named our baby for papa, Robert Themistocles, and, while at the Dills this summer, he was christened in St. Philip's Church by Rev. W. B. Howe, afterwards Bishop. Mr. Dill and Miss Hayes Rivers were his sponsors.[90]

Wallace had sold out his store at the "Bluff" to a German, George Habenicht, who also rented his land, and the last of August we returned to sister Anna's at Sylvan Home near Lawtonville & boarded there the balance of the year.[91] *Dengue fever* had broken out in Charleston just before we left, and raged until frost.[92]

When we reached ____ station on Charleston & Savannah R.R. there was no one to meet us. Wallace hired a buggy & took us to within two miles of sister Anna's, & from there we walked, arriving after night, worn out & hungry.

In January 1867, Wallace began planting operations on a *large* scale on his former plantation six miles from Lawtonville, & we moved back there. Powell was in copartnership with Wallace, and my brother Aleck was with us the greater part of the year. The latter had left home on account of the unjust treatment he received

---

[88] Mary Hayes Rivers (1811–1878) was the daughter of John Rivers (1786–1856) and Susannah Love Rivers (1786–1820).

[89] Their daughter was Regina Allison Dill (1851–1896).

[90] A St. Philip's Parish register records the baptism on August 10, 1866.

[91] This was likely George Frederick Habenicht, a native of Germany. He and his brother August were the captains and owners of ships that ran the blockade during the war. The 1869–1870 city directory for Charleston lists George F. Habenicht as a "planter" (and later as a grocer).

[92] Dengue fever is a viral disease borne by mosquitoes.

from his stepmother. He *worked hard* for his living while he was with us, but in the fall was coaxed back home by fair promises written by our father's wife, our stepmother. He was a good and noble boy, and Wallace was devoted to him. They remained always the best of friends.

During the winter (early part of '67) Georgia paid a visit to us and sister Anna and brought Annie Douglas with her. Sister Rosa & family were then living in Atlanta, Ga., where brother George & his son George Douglas had opened a large wholesale drug store, and brother George had opened an office and began practicing his profession. They flourished for a while, but were but were burnt out, lost their insurance, and were quite wrecked financially. George Douglas had recently married Lou Spencer, a lovely woman in person and character.

I did not lack for servants this year. My former excellent nurse, Mom Bess, was with me, and I had a fair cook (though a notorious thief, she was). But *cash* was very scarce, and the food procurable not of the best, & no variety, Hominy, bread & salt meat. It went very hard with me, and other things in my life were even harder to bear.

July 8th 1867, our darling little Bertie died after 8 days illness of cholera infantum, and I remained a heartbroken, desolate mother! He was buried in the old cemetery of my forefathers at Lawtonville, and there is his little gravestone.

My sister Georgia was married to Mr. Alexander E. Morgan of Tennessee August 22nd 1867 at papa's ("Blockade Place") in Screven County, Georgia.[93] We did not attend the wedding, as our stepmother did not invite any of papa's children! Georgia met Mr. Morgan in Atlanta at Dr. Douglas' house. George & Lou Douglas paid us (& sister Anna) a visit during the summer.

Our crop of cotton yielded abundantly, but the negroes depredations *were beyond belief.* They seemed to spend their entire

---

[93] Georgia (Dauda) Lawton Morgan (1845–1936) married Alexander Eakin Morgan (1830–1907), the son of John Hunt Morgan and Mary Stevens Morgan.

nights in picking & selling cotton. Several unscrupulous neighbors were buying it on the sly, among them our former kind friends, the Ayers!

Wallace could not collect the rent Habenicht owed him for James Island property ($3,000.00 had been the rent) and decided to move down & take charge himself. Besides, he had sold the plantation near Lawtonville.

1868. Early in January we moved down to James Island, going by private conveyance. Wallace tried to persuade me to remain with sister Anna, as the hardships of the journey would be great, promising to send for me as soon as he could make me comfortable, but I insisted upon going with him.

The country through which we passed was still desolate and somewhat lawless. One portion of it in _____ County had never bourne a good reputation. The inhabitants were only half-civilized, and altogether selfish & uncharitable. They refused us even the shelter of their roofs, & no amount of money or persuasion could make them relent. They seemed a species of Ishmaelites, whose hand was against every man. So we were compelled to camp out, & without a tent. A mattress was put under the largest wagon, protected on the sides as well as possible under the circumstances, & here Wallace and I slept. Brother Robert & Powell slept in the wagon, which had a canvass cover. We had one six-mule wagon, one three-mule wagon, & two in the buggy in which Wallace and I rode.

Brother Robert drove one wagon & Powell one. The times were too lawless & the negroes too unreliable to trust on such a trip, hence this arrangement was a necessity. The two wagons held our household goods. We slept one night in an outbuilding, and one night I slept in the home of Mr. Joseph Hall Waring, whose mother had adopted Wallace's mother during her orphaned girlhood & was a connection of hers.[94] It was raining hard, & quite

---

[94] Joseph Hall Waring (1823–1876) was a planter and politician who owned plantations in Dorchester County, South Carolina, called Pine Hill and

cold, but Wallace would not leave his companions, so camped out with them.

We brought food & bought food along the way, & the gentlemen drew coffee when we wished it, but most of our food was cold. Sometimes we stopped and bought a hot dinner from some farmer.

On the afternoon of the 4th day (?) we reached St. Andrew's Parish on Ashley River opposite Charleston. Here brother Robert & Powell remained with the horses, wagons, &c, while Wallace took me into the city. We crossed Ashley River in a row boat used by the Charleston & Savannah R.R. to transport passengers, for no bridge had been built to replace the one burnt during the war.

We heard that they were running horse cars in Charleston, but walked the whole distance down to Broad Street before we saw one. I boarded on Broad Street for about two weeks, Wallace being with me occasionally. He and Powell had taken the horses & other things to James Island, but brother Robert returned to his home almost immediately.

My kind friend Mrs. Dill was disappointed because I did not go to her, but I shrank from imposing upon her. While in the city I was confirmed at St. Philip's Church by Bishop Davis, who was blind at that time.

As soon as Wallace arrived in Charleston he heard that upland cotton had jumped up suddenly from ___ . Nearly the entire crop that he & Powell had made was still held by Anderson's Sons (cotton factors of Savannah). He telegraphed them immediately to hold it, but received answer that it had been sold before the rise & at the *lowest* price! So Wallace & Powell lost several thousand dollars while traveling down. (I had wished to write to Anderson *not to sell* before we left.)

At the end of two weeks Wallace moved me from the city to James Island. He then expected to our future home at Bennett's,

---

Clayfield. He was the son of Joseph Hall Waring (1784–1841) and Martha Waring (1791–1874). Winborn's mother was Martha Waring Lawton (1813–1856).

where his old home had stood. It was a lovely situation for a home, with the city in full view across the river, but there was only a *large barn* of a building there, and one negro cabin, both recently erected by his tenant of '67, and when I reached the place, I found to my horror that Wallace had not had the house cleaned up. I went to work with a will and soon had the "barn" (it had three very large rooms) cleaned up and whitewashed, and a stove set up, for it had no chimney.

We lived here perhaps a month, when Wallace decided to make a home at "Beck's Point" at the other extreme of his plantation, believing we would find health there all the year round.[95] We were mistaken!

One day about noon, Wallace rushed in and informed me that the house we were living in had to be pulled down *immediately*, as he was going to move it to Beck's Point. He had a gang of a dozen negro men waiting to fall to work. As I had no idea the house was to be moved for weeks, and not the *remotest* idea *where* we were to live while it was being moved, of course nothing was packed.

But Wallace made the men tumble the furniture and all our belongings pell mell into a filthy little negro cabin nearby, and then he went off, leaving them to demolish the larger house, and poor me, appalled and confused, to set up some of the furniture and mend the chaos as best I could.

We never did have any idea of arranging comfortably beforehand for a move, and I suffered many hardships in consequence. I had a *hard* and revolting experience while in this miserable little cabin. But we only occupied it for probably two weeks.

We then moved into our neat little house on Beck's Point. The old "barn" had been remodeled into three comfortably-sized rooms, with a piazza running along the south, and a basement below, with kitchen and storeroom. Although the place was very

---

[95] Beck's Point was located on James Island Creek, also called Dill's Bluff Creek.

plain, it was *so much* better than the others we had occupied since Sherman had burnt us out, that I was much pleased with it. I began at once setting out trees, trimming up (with my own hands) those already around us, and planning future improvements.

I even insisted upon doing the cooking in order to save all for future improvements, but Wallace objected & said that I would save very little, and lose more in other ways. And the day we moved to our new home, good old Mom Celie came to help me, and Wallace hired her to cook and wash for us.

Powell had come down from Beaufort District with us and after this, made his home with us until his marriage. He and I were always the best of friends, and very fond of each other. He was always courteous and amiable, and we never had a falling out during the time we lived together. He was very much of a gentleman in his bearing, but rather weak in some respects—poor fellow!

I led a very busy, useful life at Beck's Point until prostrated by illness in the summer. I attended entirely to the milk, setting, skimming, & even churning butter myself. I also began to raise chickens & took great delight in them. We were *real farmers* that year, and our cows, pigs and chickens were important elements in our lives. Of course Wallace & Powell planted cotton also, but the crops were not very near to our home. I also did *all* of my sewing and even made the underwear for Wallace & Powell!

I commenced keeping a diary April 7th, directly after moving to Beck's Point, & found such entries as the following *extracts*:

April 8th (1868). "Hard at work on my new Easter dress, afraid I cannot finish it in time. I have no pattern, & the new style of skirt and sacque worries me.

Saturday, April 11th. "This morning Mrs. Hinson and Fanny called and spent the morning, and *were delighted with the situation of our house.*[96] I was glad to see them, but grudged the time taken

---

[96] Mrs. Hinson was Juliana Bee Rivers Hinson (1808–1870), the wife of Joseph Benjamin Hinson (1801–1882). She had several daughters, one of whom, Frances Adeline Hinson (1846–1916), was probably "Fanny."

from my sewing. This afternoon, just as I was trying on my new dress, the Clarks called, Mr. Washie Clark, Virgie (his wife) and Lillie his sister, and Annie Baynard.[97] Virgie and Lillie rushed up and kissed me as soon as I made my appearance, & we chatted pleasantly of our school days." (This was our first meeting since we three had attended boarding school in Orangeburg together. Lillie afterwards married Dr. Frank (?) Robertson of Charleston, and died, leaving two daughters.)[98]

"The Clarks stayed until sundown and as soon as they left, Wallace sent Mr. Dill and I to town in his boat, as the ferry boat had left us. Mr. Dill and Mr. Elias Rivers arrived soon after the Clarks did. We did not reach town until after dark." (I had been invited to spend Easter with the Dills.)

12th April, Easter Sunday. "This morning I went to church (St. Philip's) early and carried a basket full of flowers from Miss Rivers to Miss [Frost]. Some of them were orange blossoms I had brought over yesterday. The church was very prettily decorated and no one had arrived except the sexton, who did not wish more flowers and tried to prevent my giving them to Miss [Frost?].[99] But I found her in the Sunday School room & gave them to her. We had very fine sermons from Rev. Dr. Miles.[100] It was rather deep for me. Mr. Dill pronounced it the grandest production he had ever heard from the pulpit! We all partook of the Holy Communion."

"This afternoon Dr. Henry Horlbeck & Dr. Lebby, Jr. called around.[101] Mrs. Dill gave us a very nice dinner. I will write the bill

---

[97] Washington Augustus Clark (1842–1931) was a lawyer, banker, and author. His first wife was Esther Virginia Melton (1845–1890), and his sister, Lydia Murray Clark (1846–1875), who is referred to as "Lillie," married Dr. William Francis Robertson (1833–1875). "Washie" was the son of Ephraim Mikell Clark (1814–1885). The Clarks lived at Ocean View Plantation on James Island.

[98] A note is penciled in here: "One Dr. T. Prioleau Whaley."

[99] A penciled note here reads: "Now Mrs. Hayne?"

[100] This was likely James Warley Miles (1818–1875).

[101] This was likely Dr. Henry B. Horlbeck (1839–1901).

of fare: Sea crabs (which I brought over for her) baked in the shell, & oysters served in milk sauce. Then a pair of fowls roasted, macaroni, and after dinner a nice bread pudding with raisins & citron in it." This was evidently my idea of a dinner *par excellence* then.

"Tonight Miss [L.] J. Holmes (Jamie Holmes) asked Mr. Dill to take her to the Roman Catholic Church to hear the 'Port Band' and invited me to go with them. He tried to make her believe he was not going & I started to take off my hat, but he & Mrs. Dill called me back. When we got to Dr. [Frost's] house (on Broad Street) Miss Frost informed Miss Holmes that 'she had a beau too!' and introduced Mr. Arthur Parker, a first cousin of hers from the country. He had the misfortune to lose an arm during the war. He sat next me in church, and took me for a young lady" (I was only 20!) "but his cousin soon informed him that I was married."

"The lady in whose pew the sexton had put us, arrived, and flew into a terrible rage at finding it filled. She stood at the pew door for some time giving us glances of steel & fire, & whispering anathemas to the lady with her. Finally she entered the pew in front, but continued to interrupt the devotions to the virgin with malicious glances at us & stage whispers. It set us all to laughing, except Mr. Parker, who wanted to give up the pew."

"We were much entertained by the robing of the Bishop. He was a stout man & seemed overcome by the heat. The Port Band did not play, but the music was very fine." (This was the first time I had witnessed these Roman Catholic ceremonies.)

(My homemade "Easter dress" was much admired by friends, and I felt quite proud of it.)

Monday April 13th. "Wallace came for me today, but it was so rough and rainy I could not go."

Tuesday April 14th. "Came over home today about midday & felt badly all the afternoon. Got my feet wet in the boat."

April 16th. "Sick with catarrhal fever, & in bed. Raining."

April 17th. "Still sick in bed & still raining. Sat up in bed & made a sun bonnet."

April 18th. "Got up this morning & overworked myself attending to milk, &c.... Am very much worried about sister Anna. Have not heard from her for 1½ months."

Sunday April 19th. "Finished writing to sister Anna & Julie. Cloudy, rainy day."

April 20th. "Mr. Dill came in while we were at breakfast and praised my butter. He & Wallace went to town together."

April 21st. "Wallace went to town again today, but forgot to mail my letters. His boat was overloaded coming back & almost sank. He brought the April number of 'The Land We Love' (a Southern magazine), being the first we've received."

April 22nd. "Wallace & I went to call on the Clarks. All at home, also Mrs. Legare and her daughter Rosa." (She afterwards married ___ Whaley and 2nd her cousin Washie Clark.)[102]

April 23rd. "Took a notion to write, and composed & wrote 'The Ocean's Lament.'" (It was a short poem on 'A Deserted Sea Island' plantation, & was published in the "Mercury," a celebrated daily paper of Charleston on September 4th 1868. I have unfortunately misplaced the paper. It was signed "Cecilia." This was my first serious attempt at writing.)[103]

April 24th. "Powell drove me over the Hinsons this afternoon & Mr. Willie Hinson showed us his bees."

April 25th. "Wallace attempted to paint his boat himself & got *full* of paint—clothes, *face* & hands. He went to town late this afternoon and took a plate of my nice butter to Mrs. Dill." (I was very proud of making good butter with *my own hands*.) "But he forgot to mail my letters again!"

April 26th. "Sold $1.05 worth of clabber & milk today!" And how proud I was!

---

[102] Rosa Susan Berwick Legare (1846–1907), the daughter of Dr. Thomas Legare and Sarah Jenkins Bailey Legare, first married John Calder Calhoun Whaley (1845–1874), and secondly, Washington Augustus Clark.

[103] The poem was published on September 3, 1868. See appendix.

Sunday April 26th. "No preaching on the island today. I read in the morning and went visiting in the afternoon Miss [Royal] Rivers."

April 27th. "Got my letters mailed at last!" (They had been written since the 19th. Sometimes, quite often, Wallace lost my letters in crossing the river, those coming to me or going to be mailed, so that my correspondence was carried on with difficulty.)

The entries in my diary record frequent visits paid & received from the neighbors, generally the Hinsons & Clarks, and to and from the Dills in Charleston. I quite frequently went over to spend the day with them, & to church, and they came over and spent the day with me. Mrs. Dill *was always good and kind*, a second mother to me.

Then there are entries of cows with twin calves, etc. & such things, showing how domestic & practical I was.

I remember of subscribing for a magazine in one of my trips to town, with the money Wallace had given me to buy myself stockings! But I concluded to darn the old ones instead. Money was still scarce down South, & everything had to bought anew after the war's destruction—houses, furniture, cattle, farming implements &c. Yet we generally had more cash than our neighbors, for Wallace was a very thrifty man.

Thursday, May 7th. "I went to town with Wallace & Powell this morning, though feeling very badly, and renounced my dower on Wallace's plantation near Lawtonville before Mr. Ned Rivers in Mrs. Dill's parlor. Ten went uptown and bought a good many things and engaged my bonnet to be made at Mrs. Wells." (She was the fashionable milliner of Charleston.) "The wind blew so hard, I had to remain in town tonight. Wallace & Powell went home. Miss Janie (Holmes) did not get home from the Citadel until after eleven, & Miss [Hayne] & I sat up for her. The officers sent for her & the other ladies in a carriage." (These ladies were doing copying for the U. S. at the Citadel & were thankful for the *per diem*, which was liberal.)

Friday, May 8th. "Wallace came up for me this morning. We had just arrived at home when Eddie Clark came to invite us to a dance at their house.[104] We all three went. Wallace would not dance, and Powell very little. I danced four or five sets" (square dances) "and also the polka, and enjoyed myself very much. Everybody was there. We reached home about 1 o'clock." (I was enthusiastically devoted to dancing.)

Saturday, May 9th. "Mrs. Dill and Gena came over and spent the day with me. I gave them calve's head soup for dinner" (how proud the young housekeeper was of this!) "and afterwards ice cream." (This was my first attempt!) "Messrs Dill, Rivers and Pelzer & son were in time for the latter, so I had quite a crowd. Was so tired tonight, I dropped asleep with my clothing on & woke up at 1 o'clock with a violent cold & minus my voice."

At this time we had services on James Island irregularly, sometimes from an Episcopal, & sometimes from a Presbyterian minister. We generally attended.

Sunday, May 17th. "Went to church on island this morning & heard a very good sermon from Mr. Prentice (Episcopal minister).[105] In the afternoon Wallace & Powell went to town to see Rev. and Mrs. Mellichampe." (Their old pastor, whom the war had driven from James Island.)[106]

Monday 18th. "Wallace brought Rev. Mr. Mellichampe over from town and Powell drove him to the Hinsons."

Thursday, May 21st. "Wallace went over to Mr. Hinson's this afternoon to make it up with the old gentleman, which he succeeded in doing." (Wallace had been suing old Mr. Hinson for

---

[104] This was Edward Bailey Clark (1853–1871), a son of Ephraim Mikell Clark.

[105] In 1868 and 1869, Episcopal minister Rev. William Otis Prentiss (1815–1897) held services in the Presbyterian church on James Island, in a new building that was completed in April 1868. The former church building had accidentally burned in 1865.

[106] This was Rev. Stiles Mellichamp (1799–1872), the rector of St. James Episcopal Church on James Island. His wife was Sarah Fowler Cromwell Mellichamp (1801–1874).

a debt he owed him, but he now withdrew the suit. William Hinson, who had assumed all responsibility, & been given all his father's property, afterwards paid him *½ the amount* & received a receipt in full.)[107] "I finished the 'Heart of Midlothian' today & am delighted with it."[108]

Saturday, May 30th. "Miss Hayse & Gena came over & spent the day with me.[109] Rev. Prentice arrived while we were at tea. Powell drove him to Mr. Seabrook's at Secessionville, and he told Powell he believed there were witches now in the world, as there was in the time of the old testament."[110]

Sunday May 31st. "Wallace & I went to church & heard Mr. Prentice preach."

Monday June 1st. "Finished making 2½ gallons of blackberry wine. Dark hen brought out 9 chickens."

Saturday June 6th. "While we were at breakfast, a lady & gentleman from John's (or Edisto) Island landed, & Wallace asked them to breakfast. They were on the way to town, had been *two days* and nights in an open row boat. Their name was Jenkins."

Saturday, June 13th. "Feeling very badly today." (I had partially recovered since the birth of my baby, and was until this period enjoying tolerably good health, but now fell a victim to malarial fever.)

Sunday, June 14th. "All three of us went to church & heard a very fine sermon from Mr. Boggs (Presbyterian) & I partook of the Holy Communion, which Wallace objected to, as it was not an Episcopal minister.[111] Taken very sick this afternoon."

---

[107] "Old Mr. Hinson" was Joseph Benjamin Hinson (1801–1882), the father of William Godber Hinson.

[108] *The Heart of Midlothian*, first published in 1818, was a popular historical novel by Sir Walter Scott.

[109] Cecilia spells the name "Hayse" several times but is presumably referring to Mary Hayes Rivers.

[110] William Benjamin Seabrook (1813–1870) lived at Secessionville Manor on James Island.

[111] This may have been Rev. George W. Boggs, who died in 1871.

Thursday, June 25th. "Sat up yesterday for the first time & the doctor (Robert Lebby, Jr.) then dismissed the case. I have been very ill with malarial fever and high temperature and suffered much. Wallace would not at first believe that it was malaria, but I got so much worse the 2nd day he had to go for the doctor, and on the way back he was taken sick himself. Both he and Powell had lighter attacks of fever while I was down. Good Mom Celie nursed me faithfully and Wallace went to town & got me a barrel of ice, lemons, biscuit, tea, &c, &c" (unaccustomed luxuries then) "& was also very kind in going out on the island and hunting up chickens, fresh tomatoes, or anything I fancied. Mrs. Hinson & daughter came to see me while I was in bed."

Sunday, July 5th. "Have been very lonely since my illness but went to town today, attended services at St. Philip's, & took dinner at Mrs. Dill's. Wallace had sent her a calve's head yesterday, and she had the soup for dinner. Mr. & Mrs. (George) Moffett and Willie Hinson were at dinner.[112] Wallace *would* not stay, though Mrs. Dill was displeased at his going. Poor little Gena (Dill) is very feeble."

Thursday, July 16th. "Wallace went fishing early this morning. This afternoon he discovered a caterpillar which he could not help showing to Willie Hinson when we drove over to Bennett's."[113]

Friday, July 17th. "Wallace went to town and showed his *caterpillar* to Fraser & Dill, Pelzer, and a crowd of others. Willie Hinson borrowed it last evening and carried it to the Clarks and those down that side. Said he never saw men so crestfallen. Nearly all in the city & country exclaimed, 'I am a ruined man!' Such a fuss over one little worm! Mr. Dill sent it to Europe." (This dread cotton scourge had appeared the year before for the first time in 21 years. No remedy was then known & the destruction it wrought

---

[112] This was likely George Hall Moffett (1829–1875), whose wife was Elizabeth Henry Simonton Moffett (1831–1897).

[113] This was an insect called the cotton caterpillar (scientific name *Aletia argillacea*), which periodically defoliated cotton crops in the Sea Islands.

was complete. Wallace took this one around in a round wooden box, with a cotton leaf to feed on.)

Sunday, July 19th. "Wallace & I went to church in town & took dinner with Mrs. Dill. Miss Cromwell (Wallace's old teacher) was also there, and Mr. George Legare & Dr. Lebby, Jr. called.[114] We did not leave the wharf until nearly dark, & had a *delightful* row home."

Friday, July 24th. "Went to town this morning with Wallace & returned midday. We were *three* hours coming home in a miserable old bateau" (belonging to some negro). "The trip made me quite sick." (Indeed, I was sick for the balance of the summer & taking quinine all the time.)

Sunday, July 26th. "Wallace & Powell went sailing in the big boat to Fort Sumter. They got home at 9 p.m. tired and hungry. Had to row home 'gin tide.' I told them, it served them right for going on a sail on Sunday."

Saturday, August 8th. "Great boat race today (sailing). Commenced at 1 o'clock. We left home at 3 o'clock and met a large crowd of people at Fort Johnson from town & James Island. The Moffetts and many of their family, the Dills, Minotts, Dr. H. Horlbeck & many others from town, & all the islanders. We had a very pleasant time (rode on the beach) and partook refreshments. Washie Clark took six of us ladies & several children in his *ambulance*" (a cheap substitute for a carriage bought at a bargain after the war), "and we had a merry time. We stayed until about sundown & all left at the same time. Elias Rivers was very *tight* & carrying on ridiculously. The gentlemen all agreed that each one who said 'caterpillar' should take a drink each time. This was to keep off the blues."

---

[114] The 1869–1870 Charleston city directory lists a Miss E. O Cromwell, a teacher, living on Church Street. She died in 1886 and was buried in the Circular Church graveyard.

Sunday, August 9th. "All three of us went to church. Mr. Law (Presbyterian) preached.[115] Everyone as blue as indigo about caterpillars. Fanny Hinson joined the church today."

Tuesday, August 11th. "Miss Julia Aldrich" (a most lovely & gentle woman, & the adopted daughter of Mrs. Hinson & sister of Judge Aldrich of Barnwell) "and Fannie Hinson spent the day with me.[116] Enjoyed their visit very much. Had chicken pie & fish & then a little custard pudding." (Simple occurrences all these, but in my old age they will help me to recall the days long past & my friends of that time.)

Wednesday, August 12th. "Wallace and I went over to Bennett's this afternoon. He hunted for caterpillars but could not find *one*. If they have not eaten him out by September 15th I am to go up the country for my health. Starling Hinson rode over to see us."[117]

Thursday, August 20th. "Spent the day & dined at the Hinsons and had a very nice day. Lillie Clark came to see me in the afternoon." They all lived at 'Ocean View' the Clarks all the year & the Hinsons in summer only."[118]

Saturday, August 22nd. "Mrs. Dill & Gena spent the day with me. Mrs. Dill brought ice & fresh beef at Wallace's request. Mr. George Chisolm came for the second time to try some 'soapy' mixture of his invention on the caterpillars as a means of destroying them. He sprays it on the plant from a large syringe. He took tea with us."

Sunday, August 23rd. "It is pouring rain. I am very unhappy in my home. I *do* try so hard to do my duty and yet I cannot get

---

[115] This may have been Rev. Thomas Hart Law (1838–1923).

[116] Julia Caroline Aldrich (1827–1882) was the sister of Judge Alfred Aldrich (1814–1897) of Barnwell County, South Carolina.

[117] Starling Lebby Hinson (1849–1902) was the son of Joseph Benjamin Hinson (1801–1882) and Juliana Bee Rivers Hinson.

[118] Ocean View Plantation was owned by Ephraim Mikell Clark (1814–1885), a planter and signer of the Ordinance of Secession. His wife was Susan Jane Bailey Clark (1814–1877).

on smoothly. Had a serious talk with Wallace about his conduct. Fever returned on me this afternoon."

Monday, August 31st. "Was sick in bed all last week with malarial fever. Mr. Prentice preached yesterday, but I was too ill to go to church."

Tuesday, September 1st. "Went to town today with Powell & took dinner with Mrs. Dill, but feeling very badly. No one came to take me home this afternoon."

Wednesday, September 2nd. "Mrs. Dill is *so* good & friendly to me, & begged me to look upon her & Miss Hayse as relatives. Wallace came up for me this afternoon and I went to bed with fever as soon as I got home."

Thursday, September 3rd. "Still in bed and quite sick. Wallace promised me positively I should go to Atlanta." (I was ill & miserable all the time. Wallace & Powell also suffered all summer & fall with attacks of chill & fever, but got off better than I did.)

Friday, September 4th. "Wallace went to town to get me some things & brought back the 'Mercury' with my poetry" (The Ocean's Lament) "in it."

Thursday, September 11th. "Feeling very badly but trying to sew & get ready for my Atlanta trip. Wallace drove me to Mr. Clark's this afternoon. Virgie is sitting up" (after birth of baby) "but Lillie is quite sick in bed...."

Saturday, September 12th. "Very busy this morning picking shrimps to take to Atlanta, as Mom Celie is sick. Old Mr. Hinson called. This afternoon Wallace took me to town. We stopped to see Mrs. Dill and then Wallace put me on the train, which started at 7:30 p.m. At last I am *en route* for Atlanta! Two nuns are on the train and I sit near & talk to them, as there are no other females. A Yankee merchant from New York took after staring so much at me that I moved my seat & drew my veil down, managed to scrape up a conversation with me. He was extremely polite & told me he admired Southern girls because of their modesty & gentleness & pictured a very *blasé* girl as a Northern type. I took occasion very soon to speak of my husband. He was perfectly amazed! Said he thought I was a young girl whom the nuns were taking to some convent" (I was only 20.) "and he had been watching me & trying to make an opportunity to warn me against them. He hated the Roman Catholics and especially their nunneries, & had built up quite a romance about one. One of the firm of George Williams & Company was on board. He found out who I was & asked me all about the caterpillars, which had now stripped the whole fields of cotton of every leaf, leaving only the bare stems."

Tuesday, September 15th. "Passed through Augusta early this morning & arrived in Atlanta 6:30 p.m." (24 hours for trip!). "Sister Rosa is in Marietta with her sick baby" (Ellie) "& brother George on a trip to Screven, but she had made arrangements for my reception, and Livie is here."[119]

Wednesday, September 16th. "Feeling very sick today. Livie wrote to sister Rosa of my arrival."

Thursday, September 17th. "Sister Rosa came over from Marietta & spent the day, but left Ellie there with her white nurse" (Josephine). "I returned to Marietta with her this evening. We reached the hotel just in time for supper. The hotel is along the railroad track, just at the station."

Friday, September 18th. "Still in Marietta, but feeling perfectly wretchedly. But sister Rosa persuaded me to go over to the hop with her for a short time. I was introduced to several gentlemen, and danced three sets, but felt too badly to enjoy them. Have met here the Habershams of Savannah and several other ladies. I like Miss Anne Habersham very much. They give us very good fare here."

Saturday, September 19th. "Sister Rosa & I, with Ellie & nurse, returned to Atlanta on 12 o'clock train. I went immediately to bed, & brother George prescribed for me. He said I had malaria and also the beginning of another trouble" (but I fought against

---

[119] Rosa Lawton Douglas was the mother of four daughters: Harriet Singleton Douglas (1858–1925), Annie Baskerville Douglas (1863–1892), Georgia Alexandra (Ellie) Douglas (1867–1957), and Rosa Lawton Douglas (1871–1972).

believing it). "Brother George left for southwest Georgia this afternoon." (He had been burnt out—office, books, instruments, &c, also his drug store, and was now travelling for a life insurance company.)

Sunday, September 20th. "Laid at home, as I am still sick. This is the 4th anniversary of my wedding. Four long, dreary years!"

Saturday, September 26th. "Livie & I went to the Democratic meeting tonight with Mr. & Mrs. [Turpin] & Dr. [Pope] walked home with Livie. Heard *very fine* speeches from General John B. Gordon (Georgia's favorite son!) & Colonel Cincinnatus Peeples.[120] All of the Democratic clubs were there & a great deal of enthusiasm displayed."

Friday, October 2nd. "This morning as I was standing on the back porch, I heard a *tremendous* crash, & looking in the direction of the sound, saw a cloud of yellow dust rising like smoke from a burning building. The fire bells began to ring, but I knew at once it must be some brick building fallen & it proved to be the grocery store of Williams Brothers (which sister Rosa patronized). We all ran down to see it. Some inmates were wounded but none were killed. One of the Mr. Williams was drenched with whiskey (from a wrecked barrel falling on him) to which the brick dust clung, & in this condition he crawled out from under the ruins unhurt. It was miraculous." (This collapse was caused by excavating for a new building alongside Williams Brother which was a two story brick.)

Sunday October 4th. "Severe chill this afternoon followed by fever."

Tuesday, October 6th. "Another severe attack of chill & fever, & suffering greatly with nausea."

Thursday, October 8th. "Missed the chill today, but fever came on in the night." (How I suffered from that terrible malaria!) "Received 50.00 from Wallace today...."

---

[120] John Brown Gordon (1832–1904) was a Georgia politician and a former Confederate general (and later, governor of the state). Cincinnatus Peeples (1816–1877) was a Georgia jurist.

Monday, October 12th. "Got up today for the first time."

Sunday, October 25th. "Went to church morning & evening with sister Rosa. Heard excellent sermons from Mr. Thomas. Received two letters from Wallace *imploring* me to return home. Answered yes!"[121]

Friday, October 30th. "Hattie & I took the train, 6 p.m., for Charleston. Brother George put us under the care of Mr. Morris on sleeping car." (The first time I had been on one.)

Saturday, October 31st. "Hattie & I got left in Augusta this morning by being locked in the sleeper. Both the porter & conductor overslept themselves. The latter tried to make amends, carried us to Globe Hotel, & showed us every attention. He went to see Misses Sedgwick" (my former teachers) "who were very kind & invited us to stay to dinner, but we returned to the hotel & left (by South Carolina Rail Road) for Charleston at 4 p.m."

Sunday, November 1st. "We arrived in Charleston 3 a.m. No one to meet us, of course, so we went to the Charleston Hotel for breakfast & afterwards drove to Mrs. Dill's. She rather expected to see us, as Wallace had been to meet us in the afternoon. Wallace arrived before dinner but was not at all well. He took us over to James Island this afternoon & went to bed immediately. He was very sick with chill & fever."

Sunday, November 8th. "Wallace has been *very* sick all the week, & doctor attending. Is not yet able to leave home. My whole time occupied in nursing him." (The curse of malaria! How it pursued us! And this was the home where we hoped for perfect health!)

We had a chimney built to our little house in November, which gave us fireplaces in our sitting room & my chamber. Before

---

[121] Cecilia wrote the following in the margin of this page (referring to the children of her sister Rosa): "I recollect Walter as then being a remarkably quiet but bright boy of 15 years, a *fine character*. Hattie as a good-natured but careless & rather lawless girl, Annie as a dear little girl of 5 whom no one seemed specially to look after, but also was always trying to tidy up her little self unaided, & Ellie as a beautiful baby. Live was my special chum while there, as usual."

this, our cooking stove in the basement had been the only means of making a fire, & had only a stove pipe. And what a time I had to get Wallace's consent! I now began to have some comfort in my home. I had improved greatly in health during the last part of my stay in Atlanta & came home quite plump & rosy. Hattie Douglas was nearly 11 years old & spent the entire winter (& part of the spring of 1869) with me. I taught her *faithfully* every day & she has since said that she learned more that winter than at all the schools put together.

We attended quite a large dance at the Hinson's summer house in November, and I wore my hair crimped and hanging down my back & about my shoulders, as was *then fashionable*! It fell below my knees, and was *wonderfully thick & luxuriant*. It was of a *dark* brown, almost black, & *very* glossy.

Wallace thought it was beautiful, & approved of my wearing it down, but Powell said a married woman should not wear her hair down.

Monday, December 21st. "Wallace & Powell left at daylight for Beaufort to attend court, but Wallace returned very unexpectedly the next day, having settled the case with Frank Johnson without going to law. Powell went on to Lawtonville."

Friday, December 25th. "Wallace, Hattie & I spent the day very quietly at home. We had some syllabubs & a few nice things.[122] Bitterly cold weather." What a forlorn Christmas it was to me!

Saturday, December 26th. "Rev. Prentice came over from town this afternoon and spent the night with us. Still very cold."

Sunday, December 27th. "Mr. Prentice preached this morning but I could not go to church as 'Amelia' could not be caught. Mr. Prentice took dinner with us & Wallace sent him back to town this afternoon." (Rev. Prentice, & afterwards Rev. Stiles Mellichampe, frequently stayed with us at this time when they

---

[122] A syllabub was a drink made of cream, sugar, and egg whites whipped into a froth and laced with sweet wine.

came over to hold services. We were almost the only Episcopal family on the island at that time.)

December 28th. "Wallace went off today & left me to have a hog killed & everything to attend to." (Though I had sometimes watched the operation on my father's plantation, I had always fled from the bloodier & more repulsive details, and I was both inexperienced & disgusted at superintending it now.)

Papa paid us a visit this winter, but stayed only a few hours. He had come to Charleston on business and & stopping at the Charleston Hotel. He wanted me to stay there with him during the several days of his visit, but Wallace objected.

1869. In January Wallace gave me a sewing machine (a Willcox & Gibbs, price $75.00 on plain walnut table with cover). I bought a lot of dainty fabrics and went to work with a will making up a "small wardrobe." Between my sewing, household & farmer's wife duties, and teaching Hattie Douglas, this was a very busy winter and spring for me.

About April 1st Hattie Douglas returned to her home in Atlanta.

Nothing of special interest occurred until April 30th, when Wallace took me over to Charleston. I had been invited by my kind friends, the Dills, to stay with them during my sickness, and Mrs. Dill now urged Wallace to bring me at once. There was no physician on James Island at this time.

We landed on high tide at the foot of Gibbes Street but I was somewhat hurt. Wallace *insisted* that I should be lifted out of the boat by June (his negro foreman). He thought this better than to get my feet a little wet, but during the night I was taken sick.

Mrs. Dill sent for Dr. Robert Lebby early in the morning & also sent over for Wallace who had returned to James Island. Saturday, May 1st I was sick & confined to my room all day, & I looked out & saw crowds of happy children hurrying past to attend May parties & picnics.

Sunday, May 2nd my second child (Alison) was born about 10:30 a.m. while the church bells were ringing joyously & the sun shone mellow and brightly. I occupied a room on the street, third story. Kind Miss Hayse wished to give me up her room, but I would not let her. This house was then #15 Legare Street (now #19). It had turned quite cool & baby wore some of George Moffett's flannels as his were not finished. The whole Dill family took the liveliest interest in my baby & were as devoted to him, & to me, as if we had been relatives.

I gave the naming of the child to Mrs. Dill (who was his godmother) & she begged me to allow him to bear one of Gena's names. Thus he was called "Alison," Gena's middle name. Mrs. Dill put "Joseph" before the Alison for Mr. Dill. ("Joseph" afterwards changed to "St. John" for my mother's ancestors.)[123]

Poor little Gena was perfectly devoted to the child and spent many happy hours playing with him. I have always been so glad I consented to the name for her sake and her mother's.

Alison was a very frail little baby at birth. Besides coming some weeks too early, the doctor said he was [born] full of malaria. His skin was transparent, for he had no red healthy blood in him. He was baptized in St. Philip's Church by Rev. W. B. W. Howe, & Mrs. Dill served cake and wine at her home & a few friends dropped in. Mr. & Mrs. Dill were sponsors & the baby behaved beautifully.

After my recovery, I boarded with the Dills the balance of the summer, for Wallace insisted upon paying board after the first month. I got through the summer tolerably well as to health, being kindly cared for by the Dills. Had it not been for spells of malarial fever that Wallace & Powell continued to have (and for one other cause), I should have been very happy.

Powell remained on James Island all summer, & at Beck's Point most of the time, & Wallace also, slept there part of the time. But continual illness finally drove them to make other arrangements, & Wallace had to come over every night. They took

---

[123] St. John Alison Lawton was baptized (as Joseph Alison Lawton) at St. Philip's Episcopal Church on August 20, 1869. He died in 1947.

most of their meals on James Island & tried the experiment of living on canned meats &c, but it did not agree with them. Wallace has always hated canned food since.

First of November found us moving back to Beck's Point, James Island. I was fortunate in having a *most excellent* girl to nurse Alison (Catherine Brown). She nursed him from a month old until he was a year & 8 months old. She went with me to James Island & I never had a better servant.

When we reached home I found that Wallace had waited until he brought me over before ordering groceries, consequently there was nothing in the home to eat except a *very little* of stale grist &c, & for 24 hours I nearly starved. He did such queer things as this sometimes, yet at other times would buy too extravagantly & wastefully. He had no judgment about such things, & would not be guided by me, though I was now developing into an excellent manager who looked ahead & provided for every emergency, if allowed to. But he often made great hardships for me.

Wallace raised hundreds of hogs, but after two or three years, had to give it up on account of the enormous number stolen by the negroes from him. "The James Island Milling Company" sprang into existence & put up [store] & cotton gins on Wallace's land at the Bluff. He charged no rent for land. Owners, Wallace, Joseph T. Dill, & William G. Hinson. They did a large business, employed a good many clerks (Starling Hinson & Callie Clark among them), but lost money.[124] Pat Gleason was in charge.[125] Wallace was persuaded to buy him out. He assumed all the debts & *thought* he had in return the "good will" of Mr. Dill & William Hinson. But the latter began opposition gins the next year, & Wallace had no *legal* papers to restrain him.

---

[124] Callie Clark was probably John Calhoun Clark (1849–1929), a son of Ephraim Mikell Clark.

[125] Patrick E. Gleason is listed in the 1877 Charleston city directory as a "salesman." A Patrick E. Gleason (1843–1890) is buried in the St. Lawrence Catholic cemetery in Charleston.

1870. January 18th. "Old Mr. Seabrook found dead in his bed this evening at his home in Secessionville, James Island. Wallace summoned to inquest."

January 23rd. "Went to church with Mr. Mellichampe (who is staying with us). Virgie's (Clark) baby died last night of croup."[126]

Saturday, January 29th. "Moved over to Bennett's this morning to our new house." (It was a sad move to me, as something happened that morning which made me miserable for many days & which I have never forgotten.)

This was decided upon because Beck's Point had proved a most unhealthy locality and was, besides, at the farthest extremity of the plantations. The house was not pulled down over my head this time, as one was built of new lumber. But Wallace's lack of managing again upset me & caused great confusion. I began gathering up and packing articles that could be spared a few days before the move, but Wallace stopped me & *insisted* upon my leaving everything for the last day, saying there would be time enough, &c, &c. Of course I obeyed him.

But judge of my confusion when he rushed into my room early before either baby or I was dressed, and telling me the boats were waiting, & the men were coming in to move the furniture, bedding, &c. I begged him to give me a short time, but he flew into a rage, then called the men in & everything was dragged out & flung pell mell into the boats & flats. Even Catherine was sorry for me.

Sunday, January 30th I recall as a lovely, almost spring-like day. I had managed to get my (little) new home into some kind of order, and I strolled out on the river bank enjoying the glorious weather & the lovely view. But my heart was heavy within me. Wallace was repentant and trying to make amends.

---

[126] Esther Virginia Melton Clark, the first wife of Washington Augustus Clark, was the mother of twelve children. Her infant son Davis Melton Clark died in January 1870. She died in 1890, and her cousin Rosa Susan Legare, who married Washington A. Clark in 1892, raised her seven surviving children.

Monday, February 3rd. "I set out 5 small orange trees in line with the old ones. Wallace set 1 large one." Yes, I went to work with a will trying to improve my future home, as I then supposed it would be. There could not be a lovelier situation. The whole city & the bay spread out in full view, and within hearing of the city's bells. The house was one story, 5 rooms & kitchen outside. Following are only notices of the building of fowl houses, setting of trees, chickens brought out, hogs killed, &c, &c, all of which I omit here. At that time I paid my cook 8.00 per month (Mom Peggy, an ex-slave of Wallace's), & my nurse Catherine 6.00 & had her washing done.

February 19th. "Wallace commenced supplying Mills House with milk." This was his first attempt at running a dairy farm, & old daddy Johnson was his head man. He sent all of his milk to the Mills House at ___ cents per quart. That hotel was crowded with Northern guests at that time & seemed to be making money.

February 21st. "Brother Robert arrived" from his home near Lawtonville.[127]

February 26th. "Went to bed with violent cold & sore throat."

Sunday, February 27th. "Wallace sent to town for Dr. Robert Lebby, Jr. He could scarcely cross the river, the wind was so high. Wallace watched the boat for two hours & thought it would be swamped. Doctor says I have catarrhal fever. He touched my throat with turpentine. My voice is gone & I have to write on a slate." This was the beginning of my throat trouble.

Sunday, March 6th. "Got up for the first time, but very weak." I did not recover my strength. Was nursing, also working very hard on sewing machine all the spring, & broke myself down. Visits to my kind friends, the Dills, continue. I & baby & nurse go over for a couple of days every now & then.

Thursday, March 24th. "Sis (Georgia) & Dade arrived this afternoon." She brought her baby, Hallie, who was about 8

---

[127] A note is penciled in over this passage: "He came to keep store."

months older than mine, & Maggie (dear old [Maner's] daughter) as nurse.[128] Georgia was then living in Tennessee, but had been visiting sister Anna.

Friday, April 1st. "Sis & I went to town upon an invitation from Mrs. Dill, & Mr. Dill escorted us to the theatre. We saw Laura Keene act, & enjoyed it immensely."

Saturday, April 2nd. "We returned home this morning to our babies, whom we had left" (for the first time).

(Dauda & I wore "Shoo-fly" bows to the theatre. They were then all the rage, & also the song of that name.[129] We had beautiful new Shoo-fly hats too.)

Saturday, April 9th. "Sis (Georgia), Wallace & I went to a large picnic at the McLeod place.[130] We carried the two babies and their nurses. There was an immense crowd there from town (Mr. Dill said a very *mixed crowd*) besides all the James Islanders. It rained at intervals all day, so that the long table had to be set in the piazza instead of under the trees. My butter, in shape of a large pineapple, was set in the middle of the table, & admired by all. (I had fixed it myself.)

"At sundown it began *pouring* in torrents & blowing hard. A rice schooner came for the town folks. Our party remained all night, & Annie Frampton (who had been very recently married) was very kind. But we were fearful of inconveniencing her & left for home *early* the next morning."

Sunday, April 10th. "We all returned home before breakfast (by boat). I found 21 of my beautiful Brahma chickens drowned in one barrel—after all the trouble I've had with them! Tired as I was, I went to church." (had a special reason)

---

[128] Georgia had a daughter named Harriet Singleton Morgan (1868–1888).

[129] "Shoo Fly, Don't Bother Me" was a popular song first published in 1869.

[130] McLeod Plantation had been the property of Winborn's half-sister Susan M. Lawton McLeod (1821–1859) and her husband, William Wallace McLeod (1820–1865).

Friday, April 22nd. "Sis, with baby & nurse left today. She took steamer 'City Point' for Savannah at 8 p.m."

Monday, April 25th. "Poor Mrs. Hinson died today, 2 p.m." (She had suffered many months with heart trouble.) "Rev. Mr. Mellichampe left this morn. Has been with us since Saturday afternoon. Mrs. Dill & Gena spent the day."

April 26th. "Attended Mrs. Hinson's funeral (at her home). Rev. Jerideau officiated.[131] Wallace sat up last night with the corpse."

May 4th. "Received letter from sister (who is now at papa's)."

Wednesday, May 25th. "Eckie (brother Aleck) arrived this morning from Screven." (Came on a visit & to take me back.)

Friday, June 3rd. "Left Charleston this evening on steamer 'City Point' for Savannah—Aleck, Dade, Alison & his nurse Catherine & I."

Saturday, June 4th. "Arrived in Savannah 6 a.m. & went to Pulaski House. Dade left at 11 a.m. on steamer 'Katie' for his home, & the balance of us at 7 p.m. via Central Railroad. We arrived at papa's about 10:30 p.m."

I remained here on a visit for almost 12 days. Baby (Alison) was very ill, pale & languid when I arrived.

Thursday, June 16th. "Arrived at Blockade Place at 12 [noon]."

Sister Rosa's family were there, & I remained for the summer, she giving me my board for my share of the place. Aleck & Robbie Oswald were both planting on the place, as we all owned a share in it, inherited from mama.

Papa had made his home here until this year, but had paid each of us (unsolicited) yearly rent (from 50.00 to 150.00 he used to send me). He had now bought a place (Oak Grove) near #5 (or Halcyondale) Central Railroad & had sold all his land adjoining Blockade Place.

---

[131] This was probably Rev. John L. Girardeau, a prominent Presbyterian minister of Charleston.

June 20th. "Brother George cut off part of my palate to relieve inflammation of the throat. He says I am in very poor health. I am thin & very weak."

June 30th. "All of us went to picnic at Mr. Crocketts."

July 15th. "Sister Rosa, Robbie & Ellie started to Lawtonville this morning." (to visit sister Anna's family)

July 23rd. "Sister Rosa & Ellie stopped at the Crockets last night (returning from Lawtonville) on account of rain. Robbie came on home & returned for them this morning."

Thursday, July 28th. "Wallace arrived this morning."

Friday, August 12th. "Wallace left for Charleston today." (Before he came, I had promised to sell to sister Rosa my undivided share of Blockade Place, but Wallace objected so strongly that sister Rosa let me off from it. This property remained a nonpaying investment for 7 years & was then *presented by Wallace to Powell*. Of course I was persuaded to sign the papers.)

Friday, August 26th. "Aleck left for Charleston today." (He went to James Island having procured a situation with Wallace, and finding that his cotton crop would not leave him any surplus, he gave his share of Blockade Place to his factor (P. H. Bohn) of Savannah) for advances.)

(I was made very sad this summer by learning that my once noble brother sometimes indulged in drinking, & I went into his room at once, threw my arms around his neck, & weeping, implored him in the name of our angel mother to give it up, & I believe he did give it up for a long time.)

Saturday, August 27th. "Sister Rosa returned from Savannah today, where she has been for 3 or 4 days, the guest of cousin Aleck (General A. R. Lawton). She had a delightful visit. As soon as cousin Sarah (his wife) heard she was at the hotel, she came for her & made her remain with her."

George Douglas came for a few days' visit to his father at Blockade. He was in such poor health that brother George would not insure his life.

Thursday, September 8th. "Left Blockade Place at sunrise with baby & nurse, & reached papa's place about 11 a.m." (Sister Rosa also was along, but she went direct to the railroad & took train for Savannah.)

Friday, September 9th. "Left papa's this afternoon & took train for Savannah. Arrived about 5 p.m. & Ned & Joe Miller met us at depot. Went to their mother (who is keeping boarding house) for the night."

Saturday, September 10th. "Left Savannah on 11 o'clock train & reached Charleston between 5 & 6 p.m. Aleck met me at depot & took me to Mrs. Dill's (Legare Street) where Wallace had engaged board." (Wallace had gone to the steamer's wharf, thinking I would probably come home by water & sent Aleck to Charleston & Savannah Railroad. At that time passengers were put across the river by a small steamer & landed at or near the west end Spring Street)

September 18th. "Walter Livingston arrived on steamer Dictator last night & went to James Island." Wallace was now running a large store & cotton mill at 'The Bluff,' having bought out 'The James Island Milling Company' (to his hurt, it proved) & gave employment to all of these members of the family.

Thursday, October 13th. "Wallace took me to the theatre. We saw 'The Green Monster,' a pantomime, acted by the Ravel-Martin Troup.[132] Wallace pronounced it *rubbish*. (Spectacular plays are just beginning to be the rage.)

Thursday, October 27th. "We moved this morning from Mrs. Dill's to our home at Bennett's (James Island). Catherine my baby's faithful nurse had found it so lonely last winter that she did not come with me. When I arrived, Wallace had not been able to hire a servant for me, & I was in very ill health. All of his work

---

[132] The Ravels were a famous French family of circus and variety entertainers who performed in Europe and the United States. A pantomime was a musical comedy production (not a silent performance). *The Green Monster, or, The Dream Fulfilled: A Grand Fairy and Comic Pantomime*, by Jerome Ravel, was published in English in 1857.

was now centered at the Bluff, but as I could not be left alone, he or Walter, or Aleck, had to stay with me. Alison also fretted the whole time & seemed sick. Under these circumstances Wallace decided to take baby & me back to town."

Sunday, October 30th. "Moved back to Mrs. Dill's this afternoon" after three dreary, desolate days at Bennett's. Up to this time Alison had not walked, but on his return to Mrs. Dill's, he was so wild with delight that, to our amazement, he stood on his feet & ran from room to room." At first we had to hold his hand, but in a very few days he was walking (or rather *running*) alone. But his ankles were weak & had to be supported by specially prepared shoes. He began to get well and plump & rosy about this time, & continued so for some years.

This good nurse Catherine came back to him & I now settled myself comfortably for the winter, as Wallace said we would remain at the Dill's. He came over from James Island every night, unless it was very stormy. But Wallace soon changed his mind & moved me back to Bennett's.

Monday, November 7th. "Wallace took Mrs. Dill & me to see Edwin Forrest in 'Richelieu.' He was simply *grand* & we were all delighted." [133]

About the last of November sister Anna & family moved down from Lawtonville & occupied our house at Bennett's. (It proved a disastrous step for all parties, in the end. She might now have owned her plantation & comfortable home near Lawtonville had she remained on it.)

Friday, December 30th. "Wallace left for Screven County via steamer for Savannah." He went on business, to collect money due from the place in Sylvania, which he had sold, & to try & make some arrangement about my share of Blockade Place.

January 1871. Wallace returned from his visit to Screven County, Georgia in a few days & at once moved me over to James

---

[133] Edwin Forrest (1806–1872) was a famous American Shakespearean actor. *Richelieu* was a historical drama written by Edward Bulwer-Lytton in 1839.

Island during the first week of January. I went with great reluctance. My health was now very poor, & I suffered much in several ways. I had been obliged to wean Alison, & he was troublesome to mind. I had no nurse, as Catherine remained in town. We had to crowd into that small house at Bennett's with sister Anna's large family. Wallace & baby & I occupied a room about 10 x 10 feet.

Sister Anna was all kindness & attention (as she always was, good soul!), but we were most uncomfortable!

Aleck and Walter both returned to Georgia about January 1st, & Aleck remained with papa & began the study of law. While we were crowded into the small house, papa & his wife came to see us, but only remained a day.

June 1st. We moved to Charleston, & with sister Anna's family occupied the house #5 South Bay (old number). I was in very poor health and not able to go out, so had a dreary (& very hot) summer of it.

Having become helpless to mind the baby before leaving James Island I hired Betsy Brown (a young negro girl) as nurse. (She remained with me for several years.)

Wallace, Powell, brother Robert & Robbie came over every night & left *very* early in the morning, rowing across to James Island.[134]

July 2nd (on Sunday) my third baby (& first girl) was born. Wallace's old family physician attended me. He gave me chloroform. Wallace, who had always declared that he wished no girl children, was *extremely pleased* with the baby & never ceased his devotion (adoration it was) during her short life. He insisted upon her being named for me, though I wished another name. Little Cecilia was very plump & healthy from her birth, but showed no extraordinary beauty until about six months old.

---

[134] A note is penciled in after this passage: "Negro riots in town July 4th." There was a very large Independence Day celebration in Charleston on July 4, 1871, almost entirely attended by African Americans, but the *Charleston Daily News* reported that it was orderly and peaceful. The newspaper estimated that about 10,000 people attended.

September first we moved to Secessionville, James Island, flying from yellow fever, which had just broken out in Charleston a few days before. Wallace at first wished me to remain & become "acclimated" (the old notion) but Dr. Horlbeck said I was almost sure to take the fever, & if I did, it would *kill me*. So we left at once. We boarded with sister Anna at Secessionville, where she had hired a large house from Mrs. Seabrook.[135]

While we were at Secessionville, the young folks had some very nice charades & tableaux at Mrs. Seabrook's. They all wanted me to represent Pocahontas, because I had such long, dark hair, but Wallace would not allow me to take the part, & when the night arrived, kept me until we got there late (it was only a few steps), though the actors sent him word they were waiting on us.

Wallace bought a very nice buggy in which he & brother Robert used to ride back & forth from the Bluff to Secessionville.

October 8th to 11th, a raging fire in Chicago which almost destroyed the city & killed several thousands people.[136] I read all the newspaper accounts & was very much harrowed up over them.

During the fall, some of us dared to go over to town (except Wallace, who said he was proof against yellow jack).[137] The fever raged with considerable virulence until almost December 1st, & sporadic cases occurred until nearly xmas, for, unfortunately, there was no killing frost. Eddie Clark (Callie's brother) died a few days before xmas, having returned to attend school in Charleston.

Wallace made a good crop this year and considerable money, as the caterpillars gave them a respite, & prices were good. He gave me anything in the way of dry goods that I wished, & from this time I dressed well & so did my children. The hardest part of our *financial* troubles seemed passed, & we always had money for the necessaries, & many of the comforts of life, after this period.

---

[135] This was likely Elizabeth Mary Royall Seabrook (1821–1900), the widow of William Benjamin Seabrook (1813–1870).

[136] This was the Great Chicago Fire of October 1871. There were about 300 fatalities, and tens of thousands of residents were displaced.

[137] "Yellow jack" was another name for yellow fever.

My future sufferings were of the *heart*, or from bad health, & a lack of forethought or care on Wallace's part to provide comforts for me. But this happened only at times, as he generally looked after my creature comfort. He *always* objected to my doing menial domestic work, & we had the best servants to be obtained always.

While at Secessionville, I was quite sick once or twice. Suffered *fearfully* with indigestion. One day I was in such *agony* that sister Anna sent note to Wallace (at the Bluff) & from the wording, he thought I had been *poisoned*. Will I ever forget that night? Dr. Robert Lebby refused to come to me. His "professional pride" had been hurt because I had employed old Dr. Horlbeck.[138]

About November 1st or a few days before, we moved to Cuthbert's house.[139] As six years had now elapsed since those 500 smallpox cases, and no one received the germs since, we decided to take the risk of living in the house. It had been a very nice house, built in the old Dutch style, and with *beautiful* grounds around it. Even after the war, a large grove of fine cedar trees encircled it, but Habenicht *cut them down* & used them for posts the year that we were up the country. Wallace threatened to prosecute him for it, but got nothing.

Wallace fixed up Cuthbert's house very nicely & bought me some good furniture, china, &c, but he neglected to build a kitchen, which proved a *great* inconvenience & caused us to sacrifice the best room in the house. It contained 4 square rooms, small hall room upstairs & a *tiny* closet under the staircase, & had 4 fireplaces & a great many windows.

Wallace took a notion that we should use kerosene stoves for cooking & bought 3 of them (cost 30.00). Such a time as I had with them! The cook nearly blew us up several times, & we had to

---

[138] This may have been Dr. Elias Horlbeck (1804–1881).

[139] According to tradition, this house was built in the eighteenth century by the Heyward family. In 1820, John A. Cuthbert purchased the property, which contained 356 acres, and it was afterward known as Cuthbert Plantation. In 1847, after Cuthbert's death, Winborn Lawton (Wallace's father) purchased the plantation. Winborn Lawton also acquired a few other nearby tracts.

have a fire besides to keep the room warm. So we soon *gave* them away, & Wallace bought an *immense* stove, much too large.

Wallace & Powell wound up, at this time, that "loose copartnership" which had existed for about five years. The terms were such that they could but cause trouble. Powell continued to work with Wallace but for *definite* wages.

January 1872. Livie Oswald was married to J. Calhoun Clark at our Bennett's Place, and went at once to his home at Ocean View, where he had a very nice & comfortable home for her, furnished & comfortable. He is such a thrifty young man, steady & amiable & a most devoted husband. (Washie A. Clark had moved to Columbia before this.)

Robbie Oswald had married in December, & soon after Livie's marriage, he and his father's family moved down to [Hineman's] plantation & engaged in planting.[140] They lost money & sister Anna's plantation near Lawtonville went to pay for advances. Robbie's wife desperately ill from time to time.

During the winter of 1871–72, I had severe chills & fever from time to time, either the old malaria, or from Secessionville, or moving to Cuthbert's before frost.

About June 1st I went on a visit to papa, taking the two babies & nurse (Betsy Brown). Remained about 5 or 6 weeks, & then returned to Secessionville. Papa has improved his house & grounds very much.

We boarded this summer July (?) to last of October at Secessionville with Mrs. Seabrook, Wallace & I, two children & nurse. Powell slept at Ocean View & took his meals with Wallace at the plantation.

Moved from Secessionville to Cuthbert's for the winter.

---

[140] Robert Lawton Oswald married Caroline ("Carrie") Vernon (1853–1893).

Epilogue

Cecilia's memoir is prefaced by a section of "Memoranda," part of which states:

> Cecilia Lawton, born Dec. 11th 1847.
> Married, Sept. 20th 1864, to W. Wallace Lawton of Charleston County, South Carolina. He was born on James Island. We were married at the temporary home of my sister Anna (Mrs. Robert Oswald) she being a refugee. None of us resided in Lawtonville, Beaufort District (now Hampton County), South Carolina, where the ceremony took place.
>
> My home was in Screven County, Georgia, his in Charleston County. Sister Anna's in the town of Beaufort, which had been captured by the Yankees.
>
> If any relationship existed between my husband & me we have not been able to trace it; yet we think there is a distant kinship.
>
> I had known him only about 2 months before our marriage.

The five decades that Cecilia lived through after she ended her memoir in 1872 had their full share of both sorrows and successes. The deaths of two of her children—her daughter Cecilia, and her son Herbert Singleton Lawton, who was born in 1874—are not recorded in her "Memoranda." Both of them died in December 1876.

Conditions for the James Island planters began improving in the 1870s after the eradication of the cotton caterpillar, and Wallace's dairy operation eventually began to flourish, but life was still difficult and sometimes dangerous for all South Carolinians during Reconstruction, during much of which the people of the former Confederate States were at the mercy of their bitter enemies in Washington, the Radical Republicans. In the second phase of this period, known as Congressional Reconstruction, the vote was for several years taken away from men who had held office in or aided the Confederacy (most of whom were Democrats). Black voters greatly outnumbered white voters, and a majority Republican government took over in South Carolina. A constitutional convention met in 1868 and produced a new state constitution, which historian David D. Wallace described as "a distinct advance in democracy," but the new state government eventually came to be characterized by extensive corruption. It was dominated by carpetbaggers (outsiders), scalawags (Southern whites who supported the Republicans), and African American Republicans, a number of whom, Wallace noted, "were the moral superiors of the average carpetbagger or scalawag, and some were of high ability."[141]

Hugh Shull wrote of the state government of this time:

> The Reconstruction government was corrupt at all levels and was responsible for stealing millions of dollars from the citizens of South Carolina by perpetrating all types of financial scams. Scams included the issuance of bonds without record of how many were sold or where the proceeds went, paper money that was issued without the authorization of the state legislature, at least initially, and the sale of worthless land at greatly inflated prices, by members and friends of the government, to the state land commission that was to be sold at favorable rates to the "landless," which included the freed slaves. The state debt increased from $8.6 million in October 1867 to approximately $20 million dollars by 1871. The majority of this money ended up in the pockets of members of the Reconstruction government and their friends.[142]

Historian Frederick A. Porcher, who lived through this period in South Carolina, called it "a story so full of horrors that it is not easy for the mind to imagine its reality." It was in some ways, he contended, worse that the war itself. Porcher recalled,

---

[141] Wallace, *South Carolina*, 573, 576.
[142] Shull, *A Guidebook of Southern States Currency*, 297–98.

Even during the war, when tidings were full of disasters and of the deaths of our brave soldiers, our minds were not so depressed as they were during a large part of the Reconstruction era. Then indeed we had the comfort of hope and the consciousness of manliness exercised in a cause dear to us; but now hope was almost gone from us, and we could show no manliness except in the fortitude with which we endured our humiliation. The country was against us and regarded with an evil eye all that we did, with a perverse understanding all that we said. The President was a fiery partisan against us, listened to no counsels except those of our enemies. Our officers were not ours, but those of our negroes; one of the Governors had said that Winchester rifles in the hands of the negroes was the best means of securing peace in South Carolina....[143]

The carpetbagger rule continued until General Wade Hampton was finally installed as governor after the election of 1876. The campaign that preceded this event was a desperate, tumultuous one in South Carolina. The Republican government struggled to keep power while white South Carolina Democrats, along with some black Democrats, struggled to oust the Republicans. There were incidents of intimidation and violence on both sides (including the intimidation of black Democrats by black Republicans) as well as voting fraud. In his biography of Wade Hampton, Walter Brian Cisco wrote of this contentious period,

> South Carolina whites believed that they had endured tyranny for a decade, that the government was plundering and oppressing them, that civilization itself was in peril. Radicals had introduced electoral fraud, their regime was propped up by federal bayonets, and corruptionists would do anything to retain power. Revolutionary methods were in order if a revolution was to be effected. Democrats would oppose force with force, backing away only when that might provoke a federal military response.[144]

---

[143] Porcher, "The Last Chapter," 181.
[144] Cisco, *Wade Hampton*, 227.

Those leading the "revolution" in support of Wade Hampton and home rule were called the Red Shirts. They were mostly members of the rifle clubs, which white citizens began forming in 1869. "In the absence of competent and consistent law enforcement," Cisco explained, "the white people of South Carolina...relied primarily on themselves for protection."[145]

In October 1876, Daniel H. Chamberlain, the Republican governor of South Carolina, issued a proclamation that the rifle clubs must disband, and that President Ulysses S. Grant would send in federal troops to enforce this measure. Five thousand U.S. troops were soon in the state. The Democrats denounced the ban on the rifle clubs, arguing that they would not have been necessary but for "the reckless distribution of arms and ammunition among the colored people."[146] There were, in fact, many well-armed black militia organizations in the state. In his recollections, William G. Hinson stated that there were three armed "colored companies" on James Island, "two of militia, one of cavalry, all well drilled by some old army men."[147]

Cecilia's memoir ends well before 1876, so we know little of what she and her family experienced during the final months of Reconstruction in South Carolina, but at least one event on James Island during this period is well-documented. In early September 1876, there was a bloody political riot in Charleston that began when a mob of black Republicans attacked two black Democrats. The agitation quickly spread to James Island, where, as William G. Hinson reported in his "Recollections," the black Republicans showed such "intense animosity" toward the few black Democrats that Hinson feared for their lives. The white residents of the island also felt threatened, and Hinson reported that they "were terribly alarmed and carried their families to the Light House on Morris Island which being government property would not be molested." There was, he recalled, "terrible excitement all night, drums

---

[145] Ibid., 226.
[146] Ibid., 235.
[147] Sloan, "Recollections by Mr. Hinson," 1.

beating, negroes collecting all about, threats and disorder."[148] The next day, rumors of the murder of three blacks by whites on the island sent the black population into greater excitement, but Hinson and another planter managed to prove the rumors false and defuse the situation, with no violence resulting.

A document that has recently come to light offers a little more insight into what conditions were like for James Islanders at the time. On October 25, 1876, fourteen James Island planters sent a petition to Colonel Charles H. Simonton, chairman of the Charleston Democratic Executive Committee, expressing their concerns about the safety of the white residents of the island. The petition stated:

> While the white voting population of the Island is only twenty-seven, entirely Democrats, the colored voting population amounts to five hundred & forty, almost entirely Republicans. By the proclamations of the Gov[ernor] of the state and of the President of the U.S. we are prevented from organizing while the colored people have a complete organization of both Infantry & Cavalry and have recently received a supply of ammunition & have shown great hostility to all who differ with them in political opinion. White citizens while travelling the roads at night have been stopped by armed bodies of colored men and as the time for the Election approaches the excitement increases and we may be liable at any time to excesses from these people without the means of affording our families protection.[149]

The petitioners asked Simonton to use his influence to have "a small detachment of U.S. troops" sent to James Island "to allay excitement and secure us against violence."

The *Congressional Record* of 1877 reveals that United States troops were indeed sent to the island, at least around the time of the election, which took place on November 7, 1876. Remarks by South Carolina Senator Thomas J. Robertson found in the *Record*

---

[148] Ibid., 2.
[149] Petition to Col. C. H. Simonton, October 25, 1876.

quote a report by Colonel Henry I. Hunt, a U.S. officer in South Carolina. In an official letter dated November 27, 1876, Hunt reported that on the day of the election he sent out detachments to various places in the Charleston area including the sea islands. An officer who was ordered to James Island with a detachment of ten men reported that he "found a feverish and excited state of feeling existing at James Island, but the presence of his command restored confidence and no disturbance occurred."[150]

During the 1870s and beyond, Cecilia and her husband continued to live in the Cuthbert house, where their only surviving child, St. John Alison, grew to manhood. Despite troubles and setbacks, the family's fortunes continued to improve, and around the turn of the century, the Lawtons moved to a house on South Bay Street (now South Battery Street) in Charleston. By this time St. John had become a partner in an architectural firm in the city.

In 1880, Wallace purchased Marshlands, a plantation on the Cooper River (in an area that is now North Charleston), and then conveyed ownership of it to Cecilia. The property was rented out for many years until she had the opportunity to sell it for a handsome price. The United States Department of the Navy wanted to establish a naval base on the Cooper River, and in 1901 purchased Marshlands from Cecilia for $50,000. That same year, she bought the Mills House Hotel on Meeting Street and renamed it the St. John Hotel. Cecilia and Wallace later lived on the hotel's second floor with their son and his wife.

Five years later, Cecilia's "Memoranda" recorded her husband's death in these words: "My dear husband, W. Wallace Lawton, died Nov. 30th 1906, in Charleston, South Carolina, at 'The St. John' Hotel, our residence on South Battery being rented out to Captain Thomas Pinckney."

In the final entry, Cecilia penned only the first three words, "Cecilia Lawton died." A side note directed, "My son, please write date, time, & place of demise & burial, C.L." St. John Alison

---

[150] U.S. Congress, *Congressional Record*, 1077–78.

dutifully completed the sentence in 1923, after Cecilia had succumbed to liver cancer: "Cecilia Lawton died February 27th 1923
about 5:30 P.M. at her residence, 43 South Battery; and was laid
to rest by her husband in the church yard of St. James Episcopal
Church, James Island, Rev. Cary Beckwith officiating."

Appendix 1

The following obituary for Winborn Wallace Lawton appeared in the Charleston News & Courier *on December 1, 1906.*

DEATH OF MR. W. W. LAWTON

After Seventy Years of Life this Well-Known Citizen Passed Away at the St. John Hotel

Mr. W. Wallace Lawton, a well-known resident of Charleston, died yesterday morning at the St. John Hotel, in the 70th year of his age. The funeral services will be held Sunday morning at 11 o'clock at St. James Episcopal Church, James Island.

W. Wallace Lawton was born on James Island, within one mile of the city, January 31, 1837, and has resided there or in the city or vicinity almost continuously. His father was a successful sea island planter, and W. Wallace Lawton succeeded him as owner of this fine plantation. The large and handsome homestead in which he was born was destroyed during the Confederate war, James Island being under military rule during the entire conflict and subject to destruction from both armies. Old inhabitants well remember the large colonial house which stood upon the opposite bank of Ashley River directly facing South Battery.

He was educated in childhood on James Island, attending private schools kept by the Rev. Stiles Mellichamp and by the Rev. Dr. Girardeau, both of whom were men of high literary attainments, and both of whom considered him one of the brightest boys of his age.

When older W. Wallace Lawton was sent to the excellent High School in Charleston, presided over by the Hon. William Porcher Miles, which at that time ranked very high both as to the moral tone and the literary standard, and which included among its pupils most of the sons of the best people of the city. Prof.

Miles took a great interest in Wallace Lawton, and always spoke of him as being very bright and intelligent.

Upon leaving this private school Wallace Lawton entered the College of Charleston, but before completing his first year there he was summoned by his father to James Island to take control of his plantation, though scarcely 17 years old. His father being blind, the entire management devolved upon this youth, who made a most pronounced success from the first. Upon the breaking out of the war in 1861, W. W. Lawton joined the Rutledge Mounted Riflemen and saw considerable service along the coast of his native State. Upon the reorganization of the company he was summoned to move his slaves from James Island to the interior by a peremptory military command, and he purchased a large plantation in upper Beaufort District, now Hampton County.

About this time he was stricken with a severe attack of malarial fever, followed by a prolonged spell of typhoid fever, which left him in an enfeebled condition until nearly the close of the war. But he continued to aid the cause in every way in his power, furnishing large quantities of provisions, aiding those men in the field by furnishing a horse to one and other needful and costly assistance to others; and near the close of the war, when Sherman's army was marching through Georgia and South Carolina and he had become stronger, he again entered the service actively, and did much scouting duty with various squads of Colcock's brigade, and also for a time was attached to Capt. E. H. Peeples's company in that section of South Carolina.

After the war he returned to his former home on the coast, to find it in the hands of the negroes, many being his former slaves. After encountering many rebuffs and insults at the hands of the United States general in command of Charleston and this district (Gen. Hatch) he, with others of his planter friends, at last got possession of their plantations on James Island, though these lands had been ruined by the ravages of war.

With unbounded energy, though very feeble for years after, he went to work to rebuild his fortune, and became one of the leading planters on the coast, taking in all improvements that could be adopted. He was one of the first to place a system of tile under-drains for his planting lands.

In all public enterprises he has always shown great interest and contributed generously; and in private there are many who will always remember his kindness.

Knowing much about Long Island (now the Isle of Palms) where he used to hunt as a youth, he took the late Dr. J. S. Lawrence there one day in a private boat from his plantation, and together they decided to purchase the island and make a summer resort of it; and when the day of payment came he generously advanced the whole sum, and continued doing so until he had succeeded in raising a company of Charlestonians to develop it, build the railroad, etc. To him, therefore, in a large measure, this community owes this now famous resort.

Appendix 2

"The Ocean's Lament" was published in the Charleston Mercury on September 3, 1868.

The Ocean's Lament
By Cecilia

(Written on a deserted Sea Island plantation.)

Sitting by the Ocean's side
Where the restless billows ride,
Where the ever-flowing waves,
From the Sea's bottomless caves,
As they dash upon the beach,
Sigh and moan, as if they each
Had a mournful tale to tell,
And sang the happy Past, a sad *farewell.*

Ceaseless billows, swelling high,
Why that melancholy sigh?
What sad tale can you unfold,
Say? And when your story's told,
I will also weep with you
O'er the dismal state you rue,
Sing me now the mournful dirge,
Whilst I am sitting, waiting on your verge.

'Tis indeed a dreary day
We are passing through; no ray
Of mirth or gladness e'er gleams,
On our broad and weary realms,
From the desolated shore,

As they did in days of yore,
Ev'ry day we come again,
Seeking a change to find; but seek in vain.

Once upon that rising hill,
Mark'd by one lone oak, which still
Stands; as if to mock the foe
That caus'd its breth'ren laid low,
Stood a noble mansion, fair,
With wide, lofty chambers, where
Cheer and sunshine ever dwelt,
And e'en the coldest temper had to melt.

From her bright, genial walls—
When the lovely Spring-time calls,
Or the moon resplendent shines,
Making many dazzling lines
On the Ocean's crested features—
Groups of gay, merry creatures
Would issue forth. Then the sound
Of mirthful laughter would o'er us resound.

Forms of beauty, want to glide
O'er our waters, far and wide,
Making all about them glad,
Now are gone; and left a sad
And dreary waste behind,
And for those, so bright and kind,
Still we sigh, mourning their stay,
Looking for them, as for the sun's first ray.

Bibliography

SECONDARY AND PUBLISHED PRIMARY SOURCES

Albergotti, William Greer. *Abigail's Story: Tides at the Doorstep.* Spartanburg, SC: The Reprint Co., 1999.

Allardice, Bruce. *Confederate Colonels: A Biographical Register.* Columbia: University of Missouri Press, 2008.

———. *More Generals in Gray.* Baton Rouge: Louisiana State University Press, 1995.

Andrews, Sidney. *The South Since the War.* New York: Arno Press, 1969.

Atkins, Smith D. "With Sherman's Cavalry." *Military Essays and Recollections: Papers Read Before the Commandery of the State of Illinois, Military Order of the Loyal Legion of the United States, Vol. II.* Chicago: A. C. McClurg and Company, 1894.

Baskerville, Patrick Hamilton. *Genealogy of the Baskerville Family and Some Allied Families.* Richmond, VA: Wm. Ellis Jones' Sons, 1912.

Biographical Souvenir of the States of Georgia and Florida. Chicago: F. A. Battey & Co., 1889.

Blackman, J. K. *The Sea Islands of South Carolina.* Charleston, SC: The News and Courier Book Presses, 1880.

Bostick, Douglas W. *A Brief History of James Island: Jewel of the Sea Islands.* Charleston, SC: The History Press, 2008.

Bresee, Clyde. *How Grand a Flame.* Chapel Hill, NC: Algonquin Books of Chapel Hill, 1992.

Broome, Dean. *History of Pierce County Georgia.* Blackshear, GA: Dean Broome, 1973.

Cate, Wirt Armistead. *Two Soldiers: The Campaign Diaries of Thomas J. Key, C.S.A., December 7, 1863–May 17, 1865, and Robert J. Campbell, U.S.A., January 1, 1864–July 21, 1864.* Chapel Hill: University of North Carolina Press, 1938.

Cisco, Walter Brian. *Wade Hampton: Confederate Warrior, Conservative Statesman.* Washington, DC: Potomac Books, 2006.

Conyngham, David P. *Sherman's March through the South: With Sketches and Incidents of the Campaign.* New York: Sheldon and Company, 1865.

Downs, Jim. *Sick from Freedom: African-American Illness and Suffering during the Civil War and Reconstruction.* New York: Oxford University Press, 2012.

"Dr. G. B. Douglas, Surgeon, C. S. A." *Confederate Veteran* 8 (1900): 83–84.

DuBose, John Witherspoon. *General Joseph Wheeler and the Army of the Tennessee.* New York: Neale Publishing Company, 1912.

Ellis, Edmund DeTreville. *Nathaniel Lebby, Patriot, and Some of His Descendants.* Privately printed, 1967.

Elmore, Tom. *A Carnival of Destruction: Sherman's Invasion of South Carolina.* Charleston, SC: Joggling Board Press, 2012.

Grinspan, Jon. "'Young Men for War': The Wide Awakes and Lincoln's 1860 Presidential Campaign." *Journal of American History* 96 (September 2009): 357–78.

Harrell, Carolyn L. *Kith and Kin: A Portrait of a Southern Family, 1630–1934.* Macon, GA: Mercer University Press, 1984.

Hayden, Rene, Anthony E. Kaye, Kate Masur, Stephen F. Miller, Susan E. O'Donovan, Leslie S. Rowland, and Stephen A. West, eds. *Freedom: A Documentary History of Emancipation, 1861–1867.* Ser. 3, Vol. 2: *Land and Labor, 1866–1867.* Chapel Hill: University of North Carolina Press, 2013. http://www.freedmen.umd.edu/LL66-67pg.html.

Hennessey, Melinda Meek. "Racial Violence During Reconstruction: The 1876 Riots in Charleston and Cainhoy." *South Carolina Historical Magazine* 86 (April 1985): 100–12.

Hollingsworth, Dixon, ed. *The History of Screven County, Georgia.* Dallas, TX: Curtis Media Corporation, 1989.

Huxford, Folks. *History of Clinch County, Georgia.* Macon, GA: J. W. Burke Co., 1916.

Johnston, Coy K. *Two Centuries of Lawtonville Baptists, 1775–1975.* Columbia, SC: State Printing Company, 1975.

———. *William Johnston of Isle of Wight County, Virginia and His Descendants, 1648–1964.* West Hartford, CT: Coy K. Johnston, 1965.

Keeley, Lawrence H. *War Before Civilization: The Myth of the Peaceful Savage.* New York: Oxford University Press, 1996.

Bibliography

Keys, Thomas Bland. *The Uncivil War: Union Army and Navy Excesses in the Official Records.* Biloxi, MS: Beauvoir Press, 1991.

Lawton, Thomas O. "The Life and Death of Robertville." *Carologue* (Winter 2000): 8–13.

Long, E. B. *The Civil War Day by Day: An Almanac, 1861–1865.* New York: Doubleday & Company, 1971.

May, John Amasa. *South Carolina Secedes.* Columbia: University of South Carolina Press, 1960.

Mehrlander, Andrea. *The Germans of Charleston, Richmond and New Orleans During the Civil War Period, 1850–1870.* New York: De Gruyter, 2011.

Miller, Annie Elizabeth. *Our Family Circle.* Hilton Head, SC: Lawton & Allied Families Association, 1987.

Mills, John, and Elizabeth Mills. *Mills-Hobby and Allied Families.* Privately printed, 1995.

Mitchell, Margaret. *Gone with the Wind.* New York: Avon Books, 1973.

Nichols, George Ward. *The Story of the Great March.* New York: Harper & Brothers, 1865.

Peeples, Robert E. H., ed. "The Memoirs of Benjamin Spicer Stafford." *Transactions of the Huguenot Society* 84 (1979): 100–105.

Poole, John Randolph. *Cracker Cavaliers: The 2nd Georgia Cavalry under Wheeler and Forrest.* Macon, GA: Mercer University Press, 2014.

Porcher, Frederick A. "The Last Chapter in the History of Reconstruction in South Carolina." *Southern Historical Society Papers* 12 (1884): 173–81.

———. "A Newly Discovered Chapter of Frederick A. Porcher's 'Upper Beat of St. John's, Berkeley." *South Carolina Historical Magazine* 117 (July 2016): 205–55.

Porcher, Richard Dwight, and Sarah Fick. *The Story of Sea Island Cotton.* Charleston, SC: Wyrick & Company, 2005.

Reichel, William C. "Historical Sketch of the Moravian Seminary for Young Ladies." *Transactions of the Moravian Historical Society* 1:10 (1876): 3–32.

Renfro, Betty Ford. *River to River: The History of Effingham County, Georgia.* Springfield, GA: Historic Effingham Society, 2005.

Rivers, Joseph L. *The Descendants of John Rivers and Ann Newman of Bermuda.* Privately printed, 2006.

————. *Seven South Carolina Low-country Families*. Privately printed, 2006.

————. *Some South Carolina Families*. Privately printed, 2006.

Rubin, Anne Sarah. *Through the Heart of Dixie: Sherman's March and American Memory*. Chapel Hill: University of North Carolina Press, 2014.

Shull, Hugh. *A Guide Book of Southern States Currency*. Atlanta, GA: Whitman Publishing, 2007.

Smith, Andrew F. *Starving the South: How the North Won the Civil War*. New York: St. Martin's Press, 2011.

Smith, Linda D. *Gare Legare: Some Descendants of the Legares of South Carolina*. Columbia, SC: Southern Historical Press, 1987.

Smith, Page. *Trial by Fire: A People's History of the Civil War and Reconstruction*. Vol. 5. New York: McGraw-Hill, 1982.

Stokes, Karen. *Confederate South Carolina: True Stories of Civilians, Soldiers and the War*. Charleston, SC: The History Press, 2015.

————. *South Carolina Civilians in Sherman's Path*. Charleston, SC: The History Press, 2012.

Taylor, Frances Wallace, Catherine Taylor Matthews, and J. Tracy Power, eds. *The Leverett Letters: Correspondence of a South Carolina Family, 1851–1868*. Columbia: University of South Carolina Press, 2000.

Trowbridge, John T. *The South: A Tour of Its Battlefields and Ruined Cities: A Journey through the Desolated States, and Talks with the People*. Hartford, CT: L. Stebbins, 1866.

United States. Congress. *Congressional Record: Containing the Proceedings and Debates of the Forty-Fourth Congress, Second Session, Volume 5*. Washington, DC: Government Printing Office, 1877.

Wallace, David D. *South Carolina: A Short History, 1520–1948*. Columbia: University of South Carolina Press, 1969.

Walters, John B. *Merchant of Terror: General Sherman and Total War*. New York: The Bobbs-Merrill Company, 1973.

Waring, Joseph Ioor. *A History of Medicine in South Carolina, 1825–1900*. Charleston, SC: South Carolina Medical Association, 1967.

White, George. *Historical Collections of Georgia*. New York: Pudney & Russell, Publishers, 1855.

MANUSCRIPTS

Agnes L. Baldwin Research Papers. Pope Family File. 0142. South Carolina Historical Society (SCHS), Charleston, SC.

Agricultural Society of South Carolina. Agricultural Society Records Minute Book. 1880–1959. 0251. SCHS.

"The Charleston Riot on 6th Sept. 1876." 34/0741. SCHS.

Hinson, W. G. Recollections. Oral interview transcribed by Annie Lee Sloan. 43/0363. SCHS.

Lawton, Cecilia. "Incidents in the Life of Cecilia Lawton." Manuscript in the possession of Robert A. Campbell, James Island, SC.

"List of U.S. Soldiers Executed by the United States Military Authorities during the Late War." M1523. In "Proceedings of the U.S. Army Courts-Martial and Military Commissions of Union Soldiers Executed by U.S. Military Authorities, 1861–1865." 1885. National Archives and Records Administration.

Marcy, Henry Orlando. Diary of a Surgeon: U.S. Army, 1864–1865. 34/0496. SCHS.

Mellichamp, Robert Elliott. "Sketch of James Island, South Carolina." James Island File. SCHS.

Orders pertaining to courts and freedmen, 1865–1866. 43/2222. SCHS.

Petition, 25 October 1876, to Col. C. H. Simonton. Private collection of James P. Hayes, James Island, SC.

St. Philip's Episcopal Church Records. Microfilm. 50-315. SCHS.

West, Mary Cheves. Statement in Reference to the Burning of Columbia. 43/2120. SCHS.

Index